THE GIFT OF THE CHURCH

The Gift of the Church

Volume 1

How the Catholic Church Transformed the History and Soul of the West

Ryan N. S. Topping

TAN Books
Charlotte, North Carolina

Cover design by Caroline K. Green

Cover image: *Giving of the Keys to St. Peter*, from the Sistine Chapel, 1481 (fresco), Perugino, Pietro (c.1445-1523) / Vatican Museums and Galleries, Vatican City / Bridgeman Images

Library of Congress Control Number: 2018947848

ISBN: 978-1-5051-0949-8

Published in the United States by
TAN Books
P.O. Box 410487
Charlotte, NC 28241
www.TANBooks.com

Printed and bound in the United States of America

The wise man will investigate the reasons of God.

~ Evagrius of Ponticus (d. 399)

Conversion is like stepping across the chimney piece out of a Looking Glass world, where everything is an absurd caricature, into the real world God made; and then begins the delicious process of exploring it limitlessly.

~ Evelyn Waugh (d. 1966)

CONTENTS

FOREWORD

> At my stumbling they gathered in glee,
> they gathered together against me;
> cripples whom I did not know
> slandered me without ceasing;
> they impiously mocked more and more,
> gnashing at me with their teeth. (Ps 35:15–16)

NEVER until these days have I thought that the psalms of suffering, and in particular those that cry out against the false tongue of the enemy, should be prayed in the person of the Church herself, our Mother. Why have I been so slow? Perhaps because I myself, in my youth, had joined now and again the voices raised up against her, or because I had taken for granted the right to carp and complain, to accept in part the old and stale accusation that the Church is old and stale, and to call that shrug of indifference by the grave name of "thought." It has been a long time since, and though the habit is gone, the failure remains—the failure to grieve with a Church so unjustly and foolishly maligned. For we would not remain silent if a mere friend upon earth should be slandered, though he were but a man as we are, and not she who rocked the cradle of our civilization, who gave us so much of what we take to be our own without her gift, and who has been given to us for our instruction, healing, and consolation upon earth, and our guide to the house of God.

Ryan Topping has not remained silent. People who were born in the oasis may take the springs and the date trees for granted. People who have wandered in the desert do not, and Topping is one of those. He has come to the oasis, and sees so much more of what the lifelong dwellers do not notice. In *The Gift of the Church*, the first of two volumes, he tells us not what his impressions are, but what is there, has been there, and, in forms that will depend upon the Providence of God, will always be there. It is, however, not merely a defense of the Church against the old slanders. It cannot be, and here I note the peculiar evil of the malicious tongue.

If a man swings his fist against me, I can parry the blow with my fist. I can answer in self-defense. No such measures are available to the victim of slander. If he stands in the square and protests his innocence, he does himself more harm than good, because he puts the slander in the ears of everyone, and while they will not remember his arguments in defense, they will remember that he had to defend himself. But if he says and does nothing, the slander puts down roots and spreads.

Thus every effective defense of the Church must be made not by the attorney but by the champion. It is not merely that your Mother has been the object of obloquy. She has been, even in human terms, the most powerful and multifarious source of good things in the history of man. Where she flourishes, man flourishes—arts, letters, sciences put to human purposes, institutions for the common good and for the alleviation of suffering, *culture* and *society* properly speaking, and where she is bound and gagged, beaten and spat upon and led among the jeering crowds, man grows sickly and sullen. He loses heart, and tries to satisfy himself with comforts fit for an intelligent beast. They disappoint him, as they must.

Topping understands this, and that is what makes this book so valuable. It is not thunder against thunder. He throws all the windows open, so that modern man in his stale little cell can breathe the fresh air of the truth again. What wonders the Church has to show us, to give us, to nourish our hearts and minds and souls, so we can be fully human again—or for the first time ever! If we need a healthy space cleared for the exercise of political virtue, not to have our deeds dictated by an imam or a servant of the emperor, well, the Church has been there before us, and gives us that space. If we wish to study the natural world and give glory to its Creator, the Church has been there, and encourages us in our enterprise. She is the Mother of sciences, the Mother of arts, the Mother of our freedom here on earth, and our builder-up for the glorious liberty of the children of God. She makes more than great men and women. She makes saints.

Read, then, and receive her gifts with a grateful heart.

ANTHONY ESOLEN

PREFACE

MY first real contact with Catholic culture was through words. My family rarely attended church. The closest thing to a religion in my background was of the Mennonite sort, and so, as a teen, it was to a Mennonite church that I went. I read J. R. R. Tolkien then C. S. Lewis and the Evangelical philosopher Francis Schaeffer, and then I stumbled upon Pascal and the *Imitation of Christ*. These pointed me to fragments of a noble tradition, sometimes called the Great Tradition, out of which the West had been built. I knew there was such a thing as Western culture. As a Protestant growing up in Saskatchewan, I wasn't sure what was left of it. I was less sure whether it was worth defending. Once I arrived at college, I encountered more words: in Augustine's *Confessions*, through Athanasius's *Life of St. Antony*, and most haunting of all, through the growling, sparkling verse of Dante. By these words I was convinced that the cultural despisers who hissed all around me—deriding Shakespeare, praising the sexual revolution, and ignoring God—were not likely to be reliable guides. Recently a friend mentioned to me a book called *How Dante can Save Your Life*, a title that captures well how I then felt about the *Divine Comedy*.

During my second year of college, I lived for a time in Eastern Europe, just after the collapse of the Berlin Wall. It was then that the architecture of Christendom opened up to me for the first time. Wandering through medieval markets, admiring the humane proportions of old squares, of streets built for pedestrians, my friends and I caught a glimpse of what life was like before the television and the automobile. I was also troubled by doubts about the past. My lessons in history had dismissed most things Catholic. Now I wondered. Did the true Church really recede beneath the horizon for the long millennium between Constantine and Luther? Was religion bound to recede as science advanced? Did progress require no-fault divorce? The Whig interpretation of our past that fed my imagination through public high school seemed all of the sudden less and less sturdy compared to the cobbled brick and stone upon which I was standing. For every good purchased by modernity, I began to count a liability. We moderns are more mobile, true, but feel less rooted; we moderns are less sexist, indeed, but find commitments hard to keep; we moderns have better health, of course, but have fewer reasons to live. I found myself gazing through Gothic and Baroque church archways wondering. I was drawn, too, by the little flickering candles inside but lacked the courage to kneel under their soft light. During the next years, these longings increased. As I dug deeper into Christianity, more and more I wanted to share the same Faith, the same culture, as Ambrose and Augustine, as Francis and Aquinas, and to enter through those archways and past the eyes of their angel-sentries less as a tourist and more as a pilgrim.

In my twenties, accompanied by my wife, I would return again to Europe as a doctoral student. At Oxford, Rome, and on Mount Athos, I came to see and hear and smell how the ancient Faith was no mere collection of stones and rituals but the living fire whose light and heat and incense had once enlivened our culture. Could it do so again? Now the words in the Great Books I read became illuminated against the backdrop of the sturdy geometry of Bernini's colonnades, the brilliant blue hues of San Chappelle's glass windows, the ruffling white and black cloth of Dominican habits, and the sonorous melodies of William Byrd's Masses. I wished not only to bow my head but also to see anew by the light of those candles that still flickered. And, by God's grace, my wife and I entered the Roman Catholic Church, a few months before the birth of our first son.

That was more than a decade ago, and we have long since returned to North America. Many folks, I am aware, find faith closer to home, as indeed I could have, had I eyes to see. Alas, in my case, I had to leave my own neighborhood to bump against it. I tell you these things now because my early experiences of beauty have shaped my approach to the study of Western culture. Over the centuries, the Church has seen her fair share of crooks. No doubt, the history of Catholicism has been marred by faithless clergy, compromised politicians, and scores of men and women who have disregarded their baptismal call. All true enough. Some of these characters find their way into the following pages. Badness is as common as it is boring. What shocks is goodness. The West's history has also been shaped by the saints, and the countless men and women inspired by their examples who have sacrificed themselves for a lofty idea, for the love of their friends, their enemies, their family, and their God.

Why should we care about the Church's influence on culture? Simply, because it points to Jesus Christ. You cannot be indifferent. Whether you trust him or despise him, whether you fear him or hope for his return, Jesus of Nazareth has been the dominant figure in our civilization for two thousand years. It is for his sake that men have fought wars and made peace; it is in his name that many curse and countless pray. We mark time by the date of his birth, and our tombstones by the sign of his death. If it were possible, with a magical eraser, to rub out from our history and our literature every story or deed bearing some trace of his influence, how much would remain? The gifts of the Church and the culture that the Church's belief has inspired are fruits born of grace and our response to the everlasting man.

This book explores and celebrates, in word and image, how our way of life—that is, the Western way of life—has been transformed and continues to be shaped by the Church's faith. For each generation, the life and teachings of Christ has provided an answer to its deepest and most probing questions. Those questions remain. So do the human longings from which they spring. Where do we come from? How shall we live? Am I loved? What awaits after death? Many of our teachers, our lawmakers, our entertainers, and even our families no longer retain the vital memory of the answers that faith offers. Through these pages, I hope to reawaken that memory. In the United States today, converts to the Catholic faith number some six million souls. Together these represent the fifth largest religious group in the nation. While many in the West are abandoning organized religion, countless Catholics and Evangelicals in North and South America, in Europe, and elsewhere are rediscovering the faith of the Church as a vital force in their lives. This book is not a doctrinal introduction to Catholicism, nor is it a work of apologetics, though I have kept both ambitions in mind. *The Gift of the Church* is, rather, an episodic account of the Church's past and ongoing transformation of the culture, the habits of thought and action, the institutions and the art, of the West. Of course, Catholicism's reach has been global. But for better and worse, the achievements of the West have drawn all other peoples into her story, and so it is here that I begin. I offer this work to those, therefore, who wish to deepen their faith with greater historical understanding and to those who look to a new flowering of Christian culture in our time.

All Christians are called to put on the "mind of Christ," as St. Paul says. But this task takes on a particular urgency for those of us who did not grow up in a coherent Christian culture or, for that matter, church family. You may have read parts of the Bible. You may even have attended services all your life. Very few of us, however, have been taught how to see the world through the lens of grace, let alone simple justice. Being presented with partial truths throughout their formation, Catholics regularly wince at the mention of Constantine's conversion, the Crusades, the Reformation, or the Galileo affair, as though history in general bore witness against the Church. Being severed from our cultural heritage, Christians often forget—or never learned—that the Church has been, and in many ways remains, at the forefront of charitable work around the globe; that she sponsors the largest international network of schools and colleges; and that she retains her status as the greatest patron of the arts.

Reading history should help us bear with the vicissitudes of fortune. It should also inspire gratitude for those and that which came before us. Remembering is one of the first duties of piety. By raising the deeds of the faithful dead, we, the living, can witness those moments when our way of feeling and acting and praying became more beautiful and good and true because of the gift of the Church in our midst. After his conversion, the English novelist Evelyn Waugh wrote that entering the Church is like "stepping across a chimney piece out of a Looking Glass world, where everything is an absurd caricature," into the real world God made. Only then, he said, "begins the delicious process of exploring it limitlessly." May these pages aid your own exploration of the gifts of the Church to our past and present. May these pages make vivid one credible Catholic point of view of the gifts of the Church to our present and our future experience of the loving God who has visited our world.

~~~

This is a tale told in two volumes. The first, and present, volume leads you through a rapid survey of two thousand years of Church history. Each chapter will introduce you to gifts given through members of Christ's body. In it you'll come to know some of the great heroes—and villains—of the West: from the early pagan philosopher turned passionate Christian, Justin the Martyr, who denounced the hypocrisy of old Rome, to the emperor Constantine the Great, whose conversion gave politics a more human face, to saintly monks who preserved the gifts of learning and
~~~

advanced agriculture to Thomas Aquinas and visionary statesmen who built universities to the tragic Luther who closed the European middle ages to Ignatius of Loyola, Bartolomé Las Casas, and their disciples who opened the modern world, developing international law and securing the freedom of slaves, to Galileo Galilei, whose clash with the Church proved fruitful for the advance of science and faith, to the clever cynic Voltaire to the saintly giant Jean de Brébeuf to the little flower Thérèse of Liseux to a sequence of popes—from Leo XIII to Paul VI to John Paul II and Benedict XVI—who have rejuvenated the papacy in the midst of a brave new world being fashioned by Marxist, feminist, and trans-humanist revolutionaries.

The second volume will extend this meditation from a different point of view. Instead of a chronological march through the history of the Church's gifts to culture, those chapters will slow down to consider the Church's transformation of particular domains. Individual chapters take up themes such as music, painting, architecture, literature, film, and the home. We will trace the origins of Western music to Gregorian chant and see how the Council of Trent and the recent interventions of Pius X helped rescue musicians from Puritanism and sentimentality; we will see why the Church has cultivated both the iconographic and the naturalistic impulses among artists; we'll explore the dominant styles of architecture that developed under the patronage of the Church (and take up the case against subjectivist accounts of beauty), witness the Church's influence on Western literary forms, consider what good popes have seen in the movies, and more. But that is all to come . . .

ACKNOWLEDGMENTS

I have many friends and colleagues to thank, beginning with those who first brought us into the arms of the Church. I thank, in particular, original members of the Emmaus House community for your friendship. In more recent years, living around and teaching at Thomas More College in New Hampshire has helped to provide our family with an immersion in the riches of a Catholic culture. We've recently returned to Canada and have already found a warm welcome from our colleagues and friends connected to St. Joseph's Seminary and Newman College.

I thank also a particular group of students. At the beginning stage of the planning and research for this book, I engaged a group of students over one Christmas break to act as research assistants, whom I here thank: Michael Gonzalez, Erin Kamprath, Ian Kosko, David Marcoe, Julie Teichert, Glenna Walsh, and Ashton Weed. Their task was to devote one hour separately to six topics I thought I might cover in the book. At the end of each hour they produced a "fact sheet" that in some cases served as a jumping off point for my research. I would also like to thank a number of friends and colleagues who read parts of the manuscript and offered comment: Andrew Thompson-Briggs, Gwyneth Thompson-Briggs, Dr. Darren Dyck, Dr. William Fahey, Paul Jernberg, Dr. Michael Siebert, and Anna Topping. Sara Levesque offered helpful editorial comments. Thanks are due also to John Moorehouse and the staff at TAN Books for their able help with this project and to Dr. Tony Esolen for writing the magnificent foreword.

I dedicate this book to Archbishop Richard W. Smith and the Sidloski family.

"You shall be called the repairer of the breach,
the restorer of the streets to dwell in." (Is 58:12)

1

PROPHETS: WHAT PAGANS AND JEWS WERE EXPECTING

"For all men need the gods."
Homer

RELIGIONS strive to explain our past. No tribe, no culture, can survive long without some plausible account of its origins. Certainly, no child was ever born an orphan. We wonder: is man an orphan? It does not help to say that before Adam was Cro-Magnon Man, nor can you dismiss the Bible by claiming that evolution provides an answer to our origins. It does not, and never could. At best, the gradual appearance of our race only kicks the question of our first beginnings back further along the road of time. Add to the end of that number of years as many zeros as you like, you still need to account for how you got the first "one." Every child, like every grown man not made childish by pseudo-science, still wants to know how he got here, the name of his father, and of Our Father.

Even so, while explaining the past is one crucial goal of religion, it is not the only or even the most important goal. Far more pressing is the task of securing hope. And here is a clue to the Church's first gift: it helped clarify a universal longing. For ancient peoples, as well as for us, religions, or at least myths, remain central because they try in one way or another to peel aside the veil that guards what is to come.

> Thrift, thrift, Horatio: the Funerall Bakt-meats
> Did coldly furnish forth the Marriage Tables.[1]

This is Shakespeare's statement of the problem in compressed form. No sooner do we become conscious of the full banquet of this life's pleasures than we feel the tablecloth being pulled out from under us. No man gets out alive. Astronomy, like biology, disappoints. Though the details of how the galaxies arose billions of ages ago rightly inspire curiosity, it is the pinch of our own impending exit from this earth that turns our hope to metaphysics, to what lies beyond nature.

This wish to steal a glimpse from the future is common to all cultures. Ancient Greeks swirled their fingers through the guts of birds. American Indians consulted shamans, and the Aztecs, the stars. In the book of Deuteronomy, we find a list of techniques that Israel's Near Eastern neighbors used in their search after tomorrow.

"When you come into the land which the Lord your God gives you, you shall not learn to follow the abominable practices of those nations. There shall not be found among you any one who burns his son or his daughter as an offering, any one who practices divination, or a soothsayer, or an augur, or a sorcerer, or a charmer, or a medium, or a wizard, or a necromancer. For whoever does these things is an abomination to the Lord" (Dt 18:9–12).

God's people were to apply to none of these aids. It is not the desire itself that the Lord condemns. It is natural for

1 William Shakespeare, *Hamlet*, Act I, sc. 2, l. 180–81.

us to want to see the future. Christians, like everyone else, habitually pray for the outcome of their battles, the health of their children, a happy death. What is forbidden is to reduce prayer to a "technology." I am reminded of the catholicity of such desires whenever I drive to my local hardware store. Along my route, about a mile from our house, a palm reader has set up shop. I pray she runs out of business, and I despise her trade, but not her. She wants what I want too: hope that the future is good. In their own way, appeals to crystals and horoscopes, not unlike insurance schemes, are exercises in risk management. In the book of Deuteronomy, the Lord does not condemn our will for security. Rather, he commands us to look for it elsewhere; he instructs his chosen people to walk down another road—the road of faithful trust.

It is at this moment in Israel's history that we are introduced to the category of the prophet. A few verses after this prohibition, we find a comforting promise. "The LORD your God will raise up for you a prophet like me from among you" (Dt 18:15). Moses offers himself as a figure of something greater to come. This promise will not be forgotten. In the first days after the Resurrection, while Jerusalem and her agitated children seethed with the news of the executed Christ, Peter preached. In his second recorded homily, he throws back at the crowd this same text from Deuteronomy. "Moses said, 'The Lord God will raise up for you a prophet.'" Surely they had heard it read a hundred times before. Every Jew had been taught to live in hope. Peter adds his own gloss: "And all the prophets . . . also proclaimed these days" (Acts 3:22, 24). The new age had arrived; the days of expectation had closed. The true prophet had arisen.

Prophets in Israel did on occasion give access to the immediate future. So Daniel interpreted dreams and Jonah predicted disasters. More importantly, though, they called the people to fidelity, and to hope. The prophets, from Moses on, are ever scolding, ever prodding, ever wooing God's people back to their senses, back to their true lover, and their covenant of love. And all of this was so that they might be ready for the Messiah. The Law, like the prophets, like the writings of the Scriptures themselves, was to prepare the people for a coming rule of peace. Certainly some hoped for a military victory over Rome. But from the beginning, it was always clear that the People of God were to look for something more sublime than a mere political revolution. God's people, and through them all nations, were to expect the coming of "the new heavens and the new earth" (Is 66:22), the harbinger of which would be the Lord himself.

~~~

From the beginning, the 611 prohibitions and commands of the Jewish law were provisional. If prophets give witness to the law, that is because law was, and still is, a necessary corrective for sin. But sin has neither the first word nor the last. In calling us back to the law, prophets point to a greater truth: man can live in hope. The creator is restoring all things to himself. History is moving somewhere: toward God's greater revelation and deeper friendship with the human family. This friendship is brought
~~~

about, definitively, through the God-man, Christ. From the point of view of their purpose, then, all the Old Testament prophesies were in some sense *Christocentric*. As the second century Church Father Irenaeus put it, the intent of God through history is the same: "there is one and the same God, who was proclaimed by the prophets and announced by the Gospel";[2] or in the words of a more recent theologian, "For the Christian, the Old Testament represents, in its totality, an advance towards Christ."[3] It's worth tracing some of those steps to Bethlehem.

The very first prophecy in Scripture is delivered moments after Adam and Eve accept the serpent's enchanting suggestion. The mother and father of our race consider themselves capable of knowledge of both good and evil. The man and woman eat and have their fill. As innocence burns away like morning mist, the Lord utters a promise for the future. To the devil, God declares,

> I will put enmity between you and the woman,
> and between your seed and her seed;
> he shall bruise your head,
> and you shall bruise his heel. (Gn 3:15)

God promises that a "seed" of the woman will crush the tempter, though not without suffering himself; the creator assures that this redeemer will be victorious, but at a cost of a bruise on his "heel." Christians, of course, early recognized this as an anticipation of the Messiah and his Virgin

---

2 Irenaeus, *Against Heresies*, ed. Alexander Roberts and James Donaldson (Ex Fontibus, 2016), 3.9.2.

3 Joseph Ratzinger, *'In the Beginning...': A Catholic Understanding of the Story of Creation and the Fall*, trans. Boniface Ramsey (Grand Rapids, MI: Eerdmans, 1995), 9.

Mother—to whom the prophet Isaiah will attest many generations later (see Is 7:14).

The next stage in the history of prophecies arrives with the opening of the covenant. After the calamity of sin, and then the first judgment of the world by the deluge, God determines not only to re-create fallen man but to leave a sign of his intent. By this sign God offers a promise to Noah: "'I establish my covenant with you, that never again shall all flesh be cut off by the waters of a flood, and never again shall there be a flood to destroy the earth.' And God said, 'This is the sign of the covenant which I make between me and you and every living creature that is with you, for all future generations: I set my bow in the cloud, and it shall be a sign of the covenant between me and the earth'" (Gn 9:11–13).

A covenant is an agreement between parties; in this case, an agreement wholly one-sided. God declares his generous interest in man. The colorful "sign" is a reminder of the promise not to destroy and, as pledge of clemency, a reason for hope. The subsequent Old Testament covenants with Abraham (see Gn 12), Moses (see Ex 19, ca. 1250 BC), and then David (see 2 Sam 7, ca. 1000 BC) will bespeak God's deepening desire to draw nearer to his chosen people and, eventually, through them, to the family of nations. Each of these covenants, like Noah's, will be ratified by signs. Thus to Abraham, God promises a nation and asks for circumcision and the sacrifice of his son (see Gn 17; 22); to Moses, God delivers the Torah on Mount Sinai and asks, on the one hand, for love of justice and, on the other hand, for priestly sacrifice (see Ex 19; 25–29); to David, the Lord promises the security of perpetual rule in exchange for friendship (see 2 Sm 7; Ps 51).

God's covenant with David heightened the Jews' anticipation for a new epoch. During the peak of his military power, and immediately after he returns the Ark of the Covenant to Jerusalem in triumph, David receives a promise from the Lord. Not only will he subdue the Philistines and every other nation that threatens the people, but through David, an heir is promised whose kingdom will have no end. "When your days are fulfilled and you lie down with your fathers, I will raise up your offspring after you, who shall come forth from your body, and I will establish his kingdom. He shall build a house for my name, and I will establish the throne of his kingdom for ever. I will be his father, and he shall be my son" (2 Sm 7:12–14).

That one of David's offspring should be called by God "my son" was suggestive. Whoever was to be this future anointed king (*messiah* means simply "anointed one") would rule unlike any other. He would be both the Son of David and a Son of God, two attributes that the New Testament writers would find fulfilled in Jesus of Nazareth (see Rom 1:3).

Not only would the rule of this Son of David last forever; it would extend over all nations. Jerusalem, as the seat of David's kingdom and the home of true worship, became from this point on the locus for Israel's messianic expectation. The city of peace, of shalom, sometimes called Zion, is the eternal city to which all can come for refreshment, even those outside of the original Abrahamic covenant.

> On the holy mount stands the city he founded;
> the LORD loves the gates of Zion

more than all the dwelling places of Jacob.
Glorious things are spoken of you,
O city of God!

Among those who know me I mention Rahab and Babylon;
behold, Philistia, and Tyre, with Ethiopia—
"This one was born there," they say.
And of Zion it shall be said,
"This one and that one were born in her";
for the Most High himself will establish her. (Ps 87:1–5)

The people did not forget this promise. Though after David's death, neither did they keep God's law.

Almost immediately after David's death, the peace of Jerusalem began to unravel. The united kingdom split again into northern and southern factions. David's beloved son Solomon "turned away from the LORD" (1 Kgs 11:9). Egypt and the rest of Israel's enemies returned in strength (see 2 Chr 12:3). The disintegration of Israel's political unity and security called into question the meaning of the promise of perpetuity. Most bewildering of all would be the destruction of the Temple and, in 587 BC, the exile of the people to Babylon, capital of the ancient kingdom that ruled the territory of modern Iraq.

It is in the immediate circumstance of war and captivity that the prophets of Israel return again to the theme of the coming Messiah. Most explicit of all the messianic prophets is Isaiah. The people had prostituted themselves before the pagan god Baal, taken on the superstitions of their neighbors, and debased themselves to such an extent that they were not above occasional child sacrifice. The prophets announced that judgment had fallen upon the people. Still, God will not forget his promise to David. A prince will be born who will restore righteousness. Isaiah's words ring out in the Catholic liturgy each Advent and, in English speaking countries accustomed to the cadences of the King James Version, with jubilant emotion in the familiar chorus of Handel's Christmas Oratorio *The Messiah*. "For unto us a child is born, unto us a son is given: and the government shall be upon his shoulder: and his name shall be called Wonderful, Counsellor, The mighty God, The everlasting Father, The Prince of Peace" (Is 9:6 KJV).

By what qualities will the people recognize their king? He will present himself as a suffering servant. He will be thought "struck down by God"; his suffering will be redemptive, for by his stripes "we are healed" (Is 53:4–5). Echoing the language of the Psalms, Isaiah proclaims that the Messiah's universal reign of peace will be centered in Jerusalem.

> For out of Zion shall go forth the law,
> and the word of the LORD from Jerusalem.
> He shall judge between the nations,
> and shall decide for many peoples;
> and they shall beat their swords into plowshares,
> and their spears into pruning hooks;
> nation shall not lift up sword against nation,
> neither shall they learn war any more. (Is 2:3–4)

After Isaiah, other prophets will fill in details. The prophet Zechariah, for instance, foretells how the Prince of Peace will come not as the great kings of old who rode on chariots but as one "humble and riding on a donkey" (Zec 9:9). He even states the precise price according to which the Savior will be betrayed: "thirty shekels of silver" (Zec 11:13). The prophet Micah predicts that the ruler "whose origin is from of old" will be born in Bethlehem (Mi 5:2). Jeremiah looks forward to the day when the law no longer stands apart from the people. During the new covenant, law will be born within the hearts of God's people. "Behold, the days are coming," promises the Lord, "when I will make a new covenant with the house of Israel and the house of Judah." This covenant will not be like the former agreements. Rather, in this covenant, "I will put my law within them, and I will write it upon their hearts" (Jer 31:31–33).

The last great prophet to speak in Israel pointed to Christ's forerunner, John the Baptist. In Malachi's closing words to the Jews, he tells them to expect a man who will make straight the paths of the Lord: "Behold, I send my messenger to prepare the way before me, and the Lord whom you seek will suddenly come to his temple" (Mal 3:1).

And then God's people enter into the great silence. It would be another 450 years till another word was spoken. No other major prophet would arise in Israel until the day that a child leaped in the womb at the sound of his cousin. Out of this silence, a child was born to a barren woman and to a man too old to become a father. The promise of Malachi would be fulfilled in the desert sermons of John. The Baptist who wrapped his body in camel skins and ate like an animal spoke words like an impatient angel, hustling his listeners into the waters of the Jordan, not so that he might take away their sins, but so they might know their need of cleansing, so they might be ready for the baptism by fire and God's own Holy Spirit. John never performed a miracle. Yet he sums up the work of the prophets. He prepares "the way of the Lord" (Mt 3:3). The night King

Herod served the Baptist's head on a platter brought to a conclusion the many thousands of years of fruitful exile of the Jews. At long last, God's people entered into the awaited reign of Jesus the Christ, son of Mary, the Messiah, Son of David, Son of God, King of Kings, Mighty God, Prince of Peace, *and* the desire of the nations.[4]

~~~

We must not imagine that such expectations were confined to the Jews. Nature breeds desire; only grace could impart hope for its fulfillment. Christ's coming, at least as the early Christians understood it, had long been anticipated by the Gentiles too. For evidence, we do not need to look far. We see this longing made articulate through the voice of pagan poets and philosophers, particularly in their yearning for two goods: everlasting life and perfect justice.

Such strange desires stalk the sons of Adam. Daisies thirst for sunshine, and there are bright days to glory in; camels want water, and there are pools from which to drink; only men desire things they cannot by nature obtain. The riddle of the restless heart, as Augustine's *Confessions* majestically describe, is the key to our peregrinations. Man is a wayfarer, a pilgrim. His aboriginal compass is his desire. Hope for future goods quickens his step all his weary days. The apostles' message was that hope will be rewarded. A dead man has risen. Christ's resurrection gives confidence in our own immortality. As the Apostle Peter

4 Helpful orientation to Old Testament prophesies of Christ can be found in Aidan Nichols's *Lovely Like Jerusalem: The Fulfilment of the Old Testament in Christ and the Church* (Ignatius: San Francisco, 2005).
~~~

argued, because Jesus rose from the dead, all the baptized have been born anew to "a living hope" (1 Pt 1:3). But, of course, it is not just any sort of immortality we seek. Life everlasting without the rejuvenating innocence of justice would be a condemnation—like the mythical Trojan prince Tithonus experienced—to an eternity merely growing *old*. Pagans wanted what Jews wanted. Even if their hope was less sure, their desires were no less certain.

The hero of the Mesopotamian *Epic of Gilgamesh* offers an early witness to this first good. The poem is a four-thousand-year-old tale of love, death, friendship, and the quest for everlasting life. As the world's oldest epic, it pre-dates both the Bible and Homer by more than a millennium. It records the adventures of a Mesopotamian king, Gilgamesh, whose name scholars of ancient Sumerian conjecture means "Old-Man-Who-Became-a-Young-Man." The *Epic* opens with an account of Gilgamesh's abuse of his subjects. Every new bride in his city, we learn, must first visit the warrior-king's chamber before retiring with her own groom. At the sight of these and other transgressions, the gods send a rival, Enkidu, a wild man more savage though less noble than Jean-Jacques Rousseau's eighteenth-century fictive ideal. The two fight and, after combat, the rivals reconcile as friends. The pair sets out on an overland adventure. They want someone or something that will offer them an opportunity to win glory. The mortals find it in a combat with a semi-divine mountain beast, which they slay, thereby earning fame but also divine retribution. The other gods take notice; they do not want competition from mortals. And so, as a punishment for the pair's hubris, Gilgamesh's dear companion, Enkidu, is killed. Gilgamesh mourns Enkidu. And it is the sight of his friend's death that launches the king upon a new and arduous quest unlike any other he has ever embarked upon, a quest for everlasting life.

Thus at the dawn of mankind, we find revulsion in the face of grim oblivion. Prior to Enkidu's death, the poet suggests, Gilgamesh had enjoyed a kind of childish serenity. His unmatched strength had delivered unreflective joy. Now, after staring into the vacant eyes of Enkidu, his power seems impotent. The dark lens of death tints his view of nature and his own achievement.

> But cruel death cuts off mankind.
> Do we build a house forever?
> Do we make a home forever?
> Do brothers divide an inheritance forever? . . .
> Dragonflies drift downstream on a river,
> Their faces staring at the sun,
> Then, suddenly, there is nothing.
> The sleeper and the dead, how alike they are![5]

In the last sequence of both the poem and Gilgamesh's quest, the hero turns from seeking fame to seeking what is more precious: knowledge of everlasting life. Distraught and disheveled, the great king in tattered cloth now wanders the face of the earth as a vagabond; he sees that his power and his land and his reputation are as straw. It is during this final hunt that he discovers "Noah" and his wife, survivors of an ancient cataclysmic flood. To this couple alone has immortality been granted by the gods. Gilgamesh wants their secret. Noah says that he will ask the gods to

---

5 *The Epic of Gilgamesh*, trans. Benjamin R. Foster (New York: W. W. Norton, 2001), 10.306–9, 312–15.

grant Gilgamesh knowledge of eternal life on a condition: Gilgamesh must prove that he can remain awake for seven days. Yet even as Noah speaks, the weary hero closes his lids in exhaustion. The poet describes a pitiful sight:

> As he sat there on his haunches,
> Sleep was swirling over him like a mist.
> [Noah] said to her, to his wife:
> "Behold this fellow who seeks eternal life!
> Sleep swirls over him like a mist."[6]

The great Gilgamesh, ruler of peoples, slayer of monsters, swimmer who has traveled across the waters of death, cannot even stay awake long enough to hear the gods whisper in his ear the secret of his longing. In this way does the oldest epic bear witness to man's persistent desire for eternity, a yearning which not even power can satisfy.

If the Sumerian *Epic of Gilgamesh* expresses a first kind of transcendent hope—for eternal life—the tragedies of Sophocles (496–406/5 BC) express the pagan thirst for justice. As the many masterpieces of Greek literature illustrate, men and women have always yearned for an unfailing moral order, a moral order that will not disappoint.

Consider Sophocles's celebrated play *Antigone*. The tragedy narrates a conflict of loyalties. Two brothers who lead opposing factions in a civil war are killed. By the end of the war, Creon emerges as the undisputed ruler of the ravaged city. As the new king of Thebes, Creon buries one brother and decrees—against religious custom—that the rebel brother's body should be left to rot exposed on the open field of battle. At this point, Antigone, sister to

---

6 *The Epic of Gilgamesh*, 11.213–17.

the fallen hero, objects. She determines to bury her brother against the law and in defiance of the king's threat of death. To complicate this tangle, Antigone is at the same time betrothed to marry Creon's son. In the end, however, she carries out her plan and is caught. The outraged king demands that his future daughter-in-law explain why she, a mere private person, should defy the public law of the city. Though she faces imminent death, she appeals to a justice that is above the king's decree: "Nor did I think your edict had such force that you, a mere mortal, could override the gods, the great unwritten, unshakable traditions. They are alive, not just today or yesterday: they live forever, from the first of time, and no one knows when they first saw the light."[7]

Antigone may not know the true source of eternal justice; yet she has no doubt that a mortal's decree cannot break it. The girl is willing to perish as a martyr for its defense.

Christians even saw pagan prophesies as pointing to Christ. The thunderbolts announcing Zeus's justice, Athena's wisdom, and even Bacchus's playful exuberance could all, in their own varied ways, be seen as foreshadowings, pointers of the true Lord yet to come. These multiple perfections would be united in the Jews' Messiah. Greeks and Romans also knew prophesies of a sort from their own canonical texts. As it happened, the most dramatic pagan prophesy foretelling the coming Christ was one given just years before the birth of the Virgin Mary by the poet Virgil (d. 19 BC). In his celebrated fourth *Ecologue*, Virgil

7 Sophocles, *The Three Theban Plays: Antigone, Oedipus the King, and Oedipus at Colonus*, trans. Robert Fagles (New York: Penguin, 1984), 502–8.

seemed to anticipate, similarly to Isaiah, a coming age of peace and the birth of a divine boy:

> The great succession of centuries is born afresh.
> Now too returns the Virgin . . .
> A new begetting now descends from heaven's height.
> O chaste Lucina, look with blessing on the boy
> Whose birth will end the iron race at last and raise
> A golden one through the world . . .
> He will receive the divine life, and see the gods
> Mingling with heroes, and himself be seen of them,
> And rule a world made peaceful by his father's virtues.[8]

For this service to the Gentiles, Dante, much later in his *Divine Comedy*, will honor the poet by taking Virgil as his own guide through hell and purgatory.

Pagan and Jew alike longed for immortality and justice; the Christian message blew the invigorating oxygen of hope onto these coals. In their address to the pagan world, early Christians sought constantly to name riddles to which the only solution was the Christ. Jesus of Nazareth was for them, to borrow a phrase from G. K. Chesterton, the Everlasting Man. He is alpha and omega, the desire of the nations. Thus, when he preached to the Athenians, St. Paul first made a careful search throughout the city to see if he might not uncover signs of incipient faith. He found them. Amid the mass of columns and merchants of that noble city, St. Paul spotted in one of their temples an altar dedicated "to an unknown god." He seized his chance. "What therefore you worship as unknown, this I proclaim to you . . ." (Acts 17:23).

---

8 Virgil, *The Eclogues*, trans. Guy Lee (New York: Penguin, 1984), 4.5–17.

Perhaps *seize* is too strenuous a term. The Athenians offered an open ear. Having long ago been freed from the duties of war by the Roman legions, Athens was by this time an easy-going university town. What these people loved above all was to sit and chat. The Bible relates how eagerly they embraced Paul. They "took hold of him" and practically dragged the Apostle to the Areopagus so that he could explain to them "what this new teaching is" (Acts 17:19).

As Paul himself would later experience, the next generations of Christians would have to make their case for living hope under more hostile conditions, even to the point of the shedding of their blood.

2

MARTYRS: THE GIFT OF WITNESS

"I am the wheat of God, and let me be ground."

St. Ignatius of Antioch

WHAT the early Christian martyrs bequeathed to the West was a model of personal sacrifice for the sake of truth. Soldiers and farmers were always willing to die for land. And philosophers had sometimes demonstrated fortitude. What the first believers proved was that heroism was no longer confined to the hero. Baptism introduced into the ancient empires of masters and slaves a new form of aristocracy, one of the spirit.

Our story begins with Jesus's living memory still in view. In AD 64, Rome, the eternal city, burned through the night. The young Nero had shown great promise. Like Alexander the Great, Nero had likewise been tutored by a famous philosopher. Up until two years previously, his old teacher, Seneca, had acted as advisor to the young emperor, seventeen years old at his ascension. His tutor was perhaps the most famous intellectual alive at the time, and a Stoic philosopher. Nero's education was confined, on order of his mother, to a primarily rhetorical education. Still, his teacher preached such noble and salutary precepts as "Excellence withers without an adversary"; "Disaster is the opportunity for true worth"; and "God hardens, reviews, and disciplines those who have won his approval and love."[1] These lines are taken from Seneca's work *On Providence*, a defense of God's justice in inspiration similar to the book of Job.

But Nero was no more a boy. Seneca's advice was no longer welcome. In AD 63, the emperor had decided he no longer required his former tutor's services. Philosophers have rarely been welcomed into the court of kings. Seneca's droning moralism now appeared a threat. Two years later, a plot against the emperor was uncovered. Though Seneca had no part in it, the threat offered Nero the pretext he needed. And so he commanded Seneca to commit suicide. Given Roman standards, the offer of such a death was actually a sign of clemency. Outrage followed upon outrage. Now, in the year AD 64, the hungry fire raged through the eternal city. While the ancient basilicas and clustered houses of Rome were melting to ash, the Roman historian Tacitus reports that men saw Nero singing. During the heat of July, the blaze crawled across the capital like a famished lion. Blame fell to Nero. Whether he actually lit the fire, he felt he needed a scapegoat. He found one in the Christians. During this first, horrendous, imperial persecution, Christians were rounded up and set as torches along the city's streets in retribution for their supposed crime.

It's as though nothing less than a fiery display could grab the attention of the capital's distracted aristocracy. These first public burnings brought Christians into the light of the

---

1 Seneca, "On Providence," in *Dialogues and Essays*, trans. John Davie (Oxford: Oxford University Press, 2007), nos. 2, 5.

Roman day. Tacitus (AD 53–130) relates the event and its consequence.

> Consequently, to get rid of the report, Nero fastened the guilt and inflicted the most exquisite tortures on a class hated for their abominations, called Christians by the populace. Christus, from whom the name had its origin, suffered the extreme penalty during the reign of Tiberius [AD 14–37] at the hands of one of our procurators, Pontius Pilatus, and a most mischievous superstition, thus checked for the moment, again broke out not only in Judaea, the first source of the evil, but even in Rome, where all things hideous and shameful from every part of the world find their center and become popular. Accordingly, an arrest was first made of all who pleaded guilty; then, upon their information, an immense multitude was convicted, not so much of the crime of firing the city, as of hatred against mankind. Mockery of every sort was added to their deaths. Covered with the skins of beasts, they were torn by dogs and perished, or were nailed to crosses, or were doomed to the flames and burnt, to serve as a nightly illumination, when daylight had expired. Nero offered his gardens for the spectacle, and was exhibiting a show in the circus, while he mingled with the people in the dress of a charioteer or stood aloft on a car.[2]

Tacitus concludes his description with the laconic judgment that "even for criminals who deserved extreme and exemplary punishment," there arose among the Roman people "a feeling of compassion." Tacitus's choice of words is telling. The generic guilt of Christians, he assumes. He accepts Nero's basic premise: their strange religion makes them "enemies" of mankind and, hence, the empire. Nonetheless, they did not light the fires. And for

---

2 Tacitus, *Annals of Imperial Rome*, trans. Alfred John Church and William Jackson Brodribb (New York: Random House, 1942), 15:44.

this wrongful accusation, there arose among the people, as he says, *miseratio*, "pity," or "compassion." The Latin word is not yet "mercy" in the Christian sense, which can be given freely and bestowed on one without merit; at this point, it expresses, at best, the beginnings of a feeling of human solidarity.

Except for brief moments, and during occasional outbreaks, Roman persecutions were not systematic. Although antagonism lasted from AD 64 until Galerius's Edict of Toleration in AD 311, and could be fierce, the intensity was never long sustained; persecutions typically were not approached with the sort of scientific rigor that contemporary totalitarian regimes have pursued their Christian and Jewish populations.

The empire was divided according to provinces. Each province was ruled by a governor who exercised discretion in matters of civil unrest and religious non-compliance to the Roman cult. Some feeling for the Roman view of persecution can be seen from the correspondence between Pliny, governor of Bithynia (modern Turkey), and the emperor Trajan. About the year AD 112, Pliny asked for direction from the emperor concerning the arrest of Christians:

> It is with me, sir, an established custom to refer to you all matters on which I am in doubt. Who, indeed, is better able either to direct my scruples or to instruct my ignorance?
>
> I have never been present at trials of Christians, and consequently do not know for what reason, or how far, punishment is usually inflicted or inquiry made in their case. Nor have my hesitations been slight: as to whether any distinction of age should be made, or persons however tender in years should be viewed as differing in no respect from the full grown: whether pardon should be accorded to repentance,

> or he who has once been a Christian should gain nothing by having ceased to be one: whether the very profession itself if unattended by crime, or else the crimes necessarily attaching to the profession, should be made the subject of punishment.
>
> Meanwhile, in the case of those who have been brought before me in the character of Christians, my course has been as follows: - I put to themselves whether they were or were not Christians. To such as professed that they were I put the inquiry a second and a third time, threatening them with the supreme penalty. Those who persisted, I ordered to execution. For, indeed, I could not doubt, whatever might be the nature of that which they professed, that their pertinacity, at any rate, and inflexible obstinacy, ought to be punished. There were others afflicted with like madness, with regard to whom, as they were Roman citizens, I made a memorandum that they were to be sent for judgment to Rome.[3]

Notice the unphilosophical character of the governor's interest. He hardly cares about metaphysics. It is the Christians' unwillingness to bow before authority that he cannot abide. Pliny goes on to relate how these executions fired the zeal of denouncers. An anonymous list of names was produced. Perceiving a threat to order, the governor inquires further. He tortures two female slaves and discovers "nothing else," as he remarks, other than "a vicious and extravagant superstition." The women had held their tongues. And now the governor looked to the emperor himself to speak. Trajan's reply gives some indication of the Roman instinct for precedent:

> You have followed the right mode of procedure, my dear [Pliny], in investigating the cases of those who had been brought before you as Christians. For, indeed, it is not possible to establish any universal rule, possessing as it were a fixed

3 Pliny the Younger, *Letter*, trans. John Lewis, 10.97.

> form. These people should not to be searched for; if they are informed against and convicted they should be punished; yet, so that he who shall deny being a Christian and shall make this plain in action, that is, by worshiping our gods, even though suspected on account of his past conduct, shall obtain pardon by his penitence. Anonymous [accusations], however, ought not to be allowed a standing in any kind of charge; a course which would not only form the worst precedents, but which is not in accordance with the spirit of our time.[4]

Romans prided themselves on their religious tolerance. They were devoted to the rule of law. And yet the spirit of the age was not so flexible as to allow a scattered fringe of devotees to a Jewish wonder-worker to publicly deny imperial pieties.

It is in the context of present or potential persecution that believers between the second and forth centuries made their defense of Christian faith. And in their apology for faith, Christians will repeatedly appeal to this natural solidarity between man and man, even as they inspired awe among their neighbors by their willingness to die for truth—a gift that the Roman world did not immediately welcome.

~~~

Pagan Rome had its own heroes. Faith in Jesus, however, ennobled every man, a point of fact upon which both Christian and pagan would eventually agree. We sometimes equate ancient Greece and Rome with Plato and Cicero. This is misleading. For most, life was brutish, short, and clouded by superstition. By offering credible hope, ordinary Christians offered to ordinary pagans a new ideal. To

---

4 "Trajan to Pliny" preserved in Pliny, *Letters*, 10. 98.
~~~

love Christ meant to defend vulnerable life and to be ready to sacrifice your own. Even enemies of the Faith had to admit the humanity of Christians.

Aelius Galenus was one such admirer. Better known as Galen (AD 129–99), this famous Greek physician and philosopher held views similar to cultured men of his class. He was not zealous in his hatred of this new superstition, nor could he discount the heroism of these simple believers. Writing a generation after the governor Pliny, Galen describes what he saw among his own patients:

> Most people are unable to follow any demonstrative argument consecutively; hence they need parables, and benefit from them just as we now see the people called Christians drawing their faith from parables and miracles, and yet sometimes acting in the same way as those who practice philosophy. For their contempt of death and of its sequel is patent to us every day, and likewise their restraint in cohabitation. For they include not only men but also women who refrain from cohabiting all through their lives; and they also number individuals who, in self-discipline and self-control in matters of food and drink, and in their keen pursuit of justice, have attained a pitch not inferior to that of genuine philosophers.[5]

What contact Galen had with Christians beyond his practice, we do not know. As the foremost medical doctor of his day, he was sometime physician to the emperor Marcus Aurelius and served also the gladiators of his native city of Pergamum in Asia Minor. Yet Galen's reference to women is instructive. That such a man who traveled in high circles should notice the experience of such socially unimportant people is striking; that such a man who traveled in high

---

5 Richard Walzer, *Galen on Jews and Christians* (Oxford: Oxford University Press, 1949), 15.

circles should admire the strength of women is extraordinary. Traditional philosophy was an aristocratic pursuit and overwhelmingly male. The philosophic religion of the Christians, by contrast, appealed to both sexes. In any case, given Galen's association with the Roman gladiatorial games, it is likely that he would have witnessed up close the death of Christians not only through natural causes but also at the hand of official Roman persecutions; almost certainly he would have been familiar with celebrated Christian deaths as well, two of which the state had orchestrated close to his home.

The first of these was Ignatius of Antioch (ca. AD 35–107), either the second or third bishop of Antioch. According to one tradition, it was during the ninth year of his reign that the emperor Trajan desired to further unite the empire by a greater conformity of worship. Christians were exhorted to worship alongside their pagan neighbors on pain of death. While Trajan was traveling in Asia Minor, Ignatius was arrested and brought before the emperor. Ignatius refused the edict, was accused of inciting others to do likewise, and then placed in chains for the long journey to Rome. Upon entering the eternal city, he would become food for the beasts of the Colosseum. In the days it took to travel there, he would be accompanied by a guard of ten soldiers; these ensured Ignatius would have the peace he needed in these final days to write a brilliant sequence of letters to Christian communities, as at Ephesus, Rome, and Smryna, where he was greeted by one Polycarp.

In these letters, Ignatius expresses unbreakable joy. His language is Eucharistic. To those Christians urging his escape, he writes, "I am the wheat of God." Like his Lord, he too asks that he might be "ground" by the beasts so that his suffering might transform him into "the pure bread of Christ."[6] Early Christian writers could be highly articulate about their own motives. Followers of "The Way" died for the sake of a message. A new covenant had been offered. No one need be excluded. They preached conversion. They proclaimed liberation for souls and wished for the transformation of the empire.

Ignatius was not the only celebrity martyr. There is a second death even closer to his living memory with which Galen surely would have been familiar: that of the saintly bishop Polycarp of Smyrna, a city a few miles south of Galen's home. Polycarp was a disciple of St. John the evangelist and a man of wide reputation. His contemporaries dubbed him "the teacher of Asia." News of the extraordinary burning of this elderly Christian leader in AD 156 would have reached the ears of even the most casual observers of political events in the region. His flesh was old, weathered by years of service. One eyewitness to the event records the spectacle of an aged body that would not burn. Upon hearing the declaration of his sentence to death, Polycarp made his final prayer and then was taken to the pyre.

> When he had pronounced this amen, and so finished his prayer, those who were appointed for the purpose kindled the fire. And as the flame blazed forth in great fury, we, to whom it was given to witness it, beheld a great miracle, and have been preserved that we might report to others what then took place. For the fire, shaping itself into the form of an arch, like

---

6 Ignatius of Antioch, *Epistle to the Romans*, trans. Alexander Roberts and James Donaldson, 4.

> the sail of a ship when filled with the wind, encompassed as by a circle the body of the martyr. And he appeared within not like flesh which is burnt, but as bread that is baked, or as gold and silver glowing in a furnace. Moreover, we perceived such a sweet odor [coming from the pile], as if frankincense or some such precious spices had been smoking there.[7]

Eventually the saint is dispatched by a sword, though not before leaving an example that would fire the imagination and courage of thousands of others who would follow him.

Early Christian martyrs gave witness to a transcendent kingdom, one which all the pomp and glory and bread and circuses of Rome could not overwhelm; the Lord himself had promised that even though "heaven and earth will pass away," his words will stand (Mt 24:35). The kingdom of Christ is present, to be sure. But its full revelation is still to come. In this age, therefore, the martyr's blood gives witness to truths that worldly power can never destroy.

~~~

If all that remained of the early Christians were such records of their deaths, if the Roman Empire would have succeeded in trampling out a few thousand coals of faith, the movement would have marked a notable moment of enthusiasm in the history of religions, though not something fundamentally unlike the myriad cults that circulated in the dying old world. If Christianity had offered nothing more than a resistance, these stories might continue to inspire in the same way that the stand of three hundred Spartans against the Persian hoard at Thermopylae does.

---

7 *Martyrdom of Polycarp*, trans. Alexander Roberts and James Donaldson, 15.
~~~

But of course the coals didn't cool. And the Christians didn't only protest. To their courage, they joined a cogent philosophy. In order for that message to be heard, they recognized that to their bloody witness must also be joined an articulate creed. At times this defense would turn to an offense, especially when directed against the mores of their pagan neighbors. In response to the charge of atheism or incest—once common slanders raised against believers—an early Christian found much to criticize in the practices of the common culture. As the fiery African lawyer and convert Tertullian (160–220) wrote:

> How many, I say, of both sorts [common men and public men] might I deservedly charge with infant-murder? And not only so, but among the different kinds of death, for choosing some of the cruelest for their own children, such as drowning, or starving with cold or hunger, or exposing to the mercy of dogs, dying by the sword being too sweet a death for children, and such as a man would choose to fall by sooner than by any other ways of violence.

You can kill us if you like, was his message – our cause is just, and justice will prevail. As he draws his *Apology* to a close, he taunts his Roman readers by saying that "the Christian blood you spill is like the seed you sow." That blood would serve as the seeds of the Church—a prediction that would be realized again and again and again in the centuries to come.[8]

Among the most memorable of these early witnesses was the Greek convert from another corner of the empire who

---

8 Tertullian, *The Apology*, trans. William Reeve, chaps. 9, 50; see also our discussion in chapters 10 and 11 of this work.

both died for the Faith and defended it with philosophical vigor. His name was Justin, later dubbed "The Martyr."

~~~

Somewhere around AD 155, Justin addressed his *First Apology* to the emperor Antonius Pius and the Roman Senate. Whether he actually delivered the text in person or it was circulated as a rhetorical piece is unknown. It didn't matter. The message reached the ears of the powerful. Justin's reputation as a debater was well established, and his taunt made him a target for future violence. Justin grew up in Palestine, possibly the son of Greek colonists. As a youth, he traveled extensively, visiting various schools of philosophy, studying, as he tells us, under Stoic, Peripatetic (Aristotelian), Pythagorean, and Platonic masters.

Unlike today, philosophy was not at that time viewed principally as an academic discipline. Nor did it confine itself to technical questions of interest to an elite class. Schools of philosophy were in this sense democratic. Men may disagree on the means, but on the end of what men seek, Aristotle had centuries earlier observed that "both the many and the cultivated call it happiness."[9] From Socrates to Jesus, that is the promise of the ancient sage. Philosophers wore distinctive dress; they gathered around authoritative teachers; they sometimes shared a common table. During this period of searching, a kindly old Christian introduced Justin to the Faith. As Justin relates, after these discussions, "a love of the prophets, and of those men

---

9 Aristotle, *Nicomachean Ethics*, trans. Terence Irwin, 1.4.2.
~~~

who are friends of Christ, possessed me."[10] Christianity, for Justin, represented the fulfillment of his quest for wisdom; faith was the consummation of philosophy.

Justin's strategy before the emperor was ingenious. He took up and dismissed charges then commonly laid against these people of "the Way." "No, we are not atheists"; "we do not sacrifice our children"; "we are loyal to the state" is the gist of his message. He showed how Christ fulfills Old Testament prophecies. Then he turned to philosophy. In Greek—still at this time the language of the empire—the term *logos* could mean "reason," "word," or simply "speech." St. John, at the opening of his Gospel, grabbed a cup from the common man's table and filled this ordinary vessel with an uncommon sense. *Logos* gave a name to God's generosity. "And the Word [*logos*] became flesh," the apostle wrote, "and dwelt among us" (Jn 1:14). He who enjoyed everlasting union with the Father, the divine idea, he who is the primordial thought, the speechless Word from eternity, confined himself to space and time. Reason now wore a face.

Drawing upon his philosophical training, Justin pressed his case. Flesh and blood had never lived without this Reason. Indeed, those sages of any age who loved the truth were guided by Christ, the divine logos. Some even deserved to share the name of Christian. Among these, Justin brought into the Christian circle Socrates, Heraclitus, "and people like them."[11] At a stroke, this convert gathered into the family of the Church everyone and everything about classical

---

10 Justin Martyr, *Dialogue with Trypho*, trans. Alexander Roberts and James Donaldson, 8.

11 Justin Martyr, *First Apology*, trans. Leslie William Barnard, 46.

antiquity, and every other kind of antiquity, that was true and good. The future belonged to the Faith. This same Jesus whom Hebrew prophets foretold was the one eternal Word who enlightened lovers of wisdom now and always. The Christian need not leave behind anything beautiful.

~~~

It is true that not all Christians have been warm to Justin's way of reasoning. During the Protestant Reformation, and then again in the nineteenth century, scholars tried to abstract the original, primitive message of the Gospel from its later, Greco-Roman-influenced presentation. Luther famously quipped, "Aristotle is to theology as darkness is to light."[12] Whenever theologians borrow from philosophers, in other words, they devalue their own proper currency. Justin would have disagreed. So would the broad consensus of theologians that came after him. Tension between revelation and reason has always been present within the Christian tradition, but, overwhelmingly, this has been experienced as a creative and not a destructive force. God, as Augustine will later say, has given us "two books" from which to read his mind: Scripture and nature. Since the author of both is one and the same, the two messages can never conflict. During his confrontation with certain churchmen at the dawn of the modern era, Galileo quoted extensively from St. Augustine's *Literal Commentary on Genesis* to make the same point, and included this

---

12 Martin Luther, *Disputation Against Scholastic Theology*, proposition 50 in *Luther's Works,* ed. H. Grimm, vol. 31, *Career of the Reformer,* I, 12.
~~~

quip from a contemporary theologian, Cardinal Baronius (1538–1607), to silence his critics: "the intention of the Holy Spirit is to teach us how one goes to heaven and not how heaven goes."[13]

Martyrdom was not the same thing as mere fanaticism. As we shall explore later, this openness to inquiry, this confidence in the essential goodness of reason, and the inherent reasonability of the martyr's message are also what substantially account for the West's development of the universities in the thirteenth century, the rise of modern science in the seventeenth century, and the fight against totalitarianism in the twentieth century. Ancient cultures of the East had no corresponding conception of the eternal logos. Nor does Islam. The friendship of faith and reason is among the Church's distinctive gifts to the West, and it is a friendship that has been expressed through both word and deed. The life of Justin can be considered one of its first fruits. As Pope Benedict XVI explained in his 2006 "Regensburg Address," "This inner rapprochement between Biblical faith and Greek philosophical inquiry was an event of decisive importance not only from the standpoint of the history of religions, but also from that of world history."

And yet, for all his erudition, Justin is not chiefly remembered as a thinker. He is remembered as one who shed his blood for Christ, as "the martyr." Just as Christ sacrificed himself for us, so his disciples must sacrifice themselves for others. We know the end of his story. About a decade

---

13 Galileo, "Letter to Christiana" in *The Galileo Affair: A Documentary History*, ed. and trans. M. Finocchiaro, 96.

after his defense before the emperor, Justin would be hauled before Rusticus, prefect of the city of Rome. Some speculated that his arrest was orchestrated by Crescens, a pagan philosopher with whom Justin had previously argued and likely conquered in public debate. However he was betrayed, the earliest accounts sketch the broad outlines of how he met his end in 165, about a century after Rome's great fire. Justin and a group of companions were commanded to sacrifice to the gods of the imperial state. Justin refused. He and his friends were beaten with rods. They continued to praise Christ and were beheaded.

Justin's vigorous witness cost him his earthly life, though that did not really end his story. His death won for the Church and the West a victory far greater than either emperor or senator could have then imagined. If in truth the blood of the martyrs pours forth the seeds of the Church, Justin's defense was unimaginably fruitful. Wherever Christians have made their presence felt, they have brought with them a devotion to truth and, through their martyrs, a willingness to die for a kingdom that will outlast all the governments of this world.

Fewer than two hundred years later, another emperor would heed the message of the martyrs and bend his knee before Justin's Lord. As the Church and the West would soon discover, the conversion of empires would bring its own complications and rain down upon Christians both blessings and curses, and the need to grope toward distinctions. In the coming centuries, the Church would learn, through many painful lessons, what it meant to separate the things that belong to Caesar from the things that belong to Christ.

3

CONSTANTINE: GIFTS TO GOD AND CAESAR

"And truly may he deserve the imperial title, who has formed his soul to royal virtues."

Bishop Eusebius of Caesarea

IT is common these days to rejoice at the collapse of Christendom. The medieval Church was too closely bound up with power, some people say. Safer for all sides, others insist, would it be to enforce an impenetrable wall between things religious and things temporal. Popes might even be taken to support such a view. In a dramatic act of renunciation in 1963, Blessed Paul VI sold the papal tiara—his sign of temporal authority—and gave the money to charity. The common judgment against our past is, I think, partially right. It is better that bishops no longer busy themselves resolving conflicts over, say, land titles. Where our judgment seems confused, however, is when it leads us to forget that the *idea* of the separation of Church from State is an ancient Catholic innovation. No one, neither Pericles's Greeks nor Cicero's Romans nor the Chinese nor the Muslims had ever conceived of the principled separation of powers. The notion that power should be divided between a secular and a spiritual authority—even within a religiously unified realm—is a truth the Church has jealously guarded even as it has applied the principle variously according to changing circumstances, from the times of Constantine to the investiture controversies of the twelfth century to the wrangling over education in nineteenth-century France to the legal battles over the independence of Catholic hospitals and adoption agencies in contemporary North America.

The Church's recurring defense of this principle is forgotten by many modern Catholics.[1] Distinction need not imply hostile separation. One can be glad that the Vatican no longer commands mercenary armies without conceding that she should lose interest in how militaries define their rules of engagement. Indeed, the Church has never conceded a sphere of activity to be wholly alien from Christ. The Second Vatican Council did not encourage secularism, so defined. To the contrary, when speaking of the task of the laity, the bishops declared that "God's plan for the world is that men should work together to renew and constantly perfect the temporal order."[2] This just aspiration has animated the work of every pious Christian ruler since Constantine the Great.

---

1 On the modern Church's view of her work in relation to politics, I point to three reflections: Regis Scanlon, "Did Vatican II Reverse the Church's teaching on Religious Liberty," *Homiletic and Pastoral Review* (January 2011): 61–68; F. Russell Hittinger, "The Declaration on Religious Freedom, *Dignitatis Humane*," in *Vatican II: Renewal Within Tradition*, eds. Matthew Lamb and Matthew Levering (Oxford: OUP, 2008); and Douglas Farrow, "Catholics and the Neutral State," in *Desiring a Better Country: Forays in Political Theology* (Montreal: McGill-Queens, 2015).

2 Pope Paul VI, *Apostolicam Actuositatem* (1965), 7.

Popular accounts of the West's first Christian emperor tend toward cynicism. One recent description of Constantine the Great's contribution to the formation of the Bible draws this startling conclusion:

> [Sir Leigh Teabing]: "More than eighty gospels were considered for the New Testament, and yet only a relative few were chosen for inclusions—Matthew, Mark, Luke and John among them."
>
> "Who chose which gospels to include?" Sophie asked. "Aha!" Teabing burst in with enthusiasm. "The fundamental irony of Christianity! The Bible, as we know it today, was collated by the pagan Roman Emperor Constantine the Great."[3]

Remarkable irony indeed! If true, such would put Constantine higher than the Apostles, second only to Jesus Christ himself. Of course, this claim, like much else in Dan Brown's *The Da Vinci Code*, is almost entirely untrue. Sadly, for thousands of our contemporaries, such accounts serve as a guide to the legacy of Constantine and the consequence of his sword.

Let us set aside, for a moment, concern for truth; from the point of view of artistic taste alone, this muddling of people's minds is a pity. Some ages, no doubt, have been dull. Not so the fourth century. In this case, the truth is eminently more interesting than fiction. That span of one hundred years (AD 310–410) saw the end of brutal persecution, the consolidation of Church doctrine, the first steps toward the conversion of the barbarian kings, and a fruitful new relationship between the rulers of this world and

---

3 Dan Brown, *The Da Vinci Code: A Novel* (New York: Anchor Books, 2003), 304.

the kingdom of Christ. Through Constantine's legacy, the Church gave the West two enduring gifts: a pattern of religiously motivated secular service and the principled distinction between the offices of Church and State.

War was inevitable. At the death of Constantine's father, Constantius (the Pale-faced), Constantine's troops had proclaimed Constantine "Augustus" while on campaign in the northern province of Britain at York. The emperor Diocletian had recently divided authority over Rome's vast territory between four rulers, or tetrarchs, as they were called. It was a reasonable division. Two senior "Augusti," in theory, were to be succeeded by two younger commanders, designated "Caesars." But the balance did not long survive. Rome had suffered a century of political setbacks. The prestige of the Senate waned. Within living memory, emperors had been established and deposed as quickly as college football coaches are today. Ambition was set against ambition. Upon learning of the treasonable plans of his co-ruler, Maxentius, Constantine turned his face against his competitor and toward Rome.

Constantine's men were better trained. They were also outnumbered by nearly two to one. One estimate puts Constantine's 90,000 soldiers and 8,000 horse against Maxentius's 170,000 foot soldiers and 18,000 cavalry. Through Gaul and along the alpine passes of Italy, the disciplined mass of steel and horse rattled day after day, pounding the earth as they traveled south on their errand of death. Then came the vision. One afternoon, under open sky, Constantine and his men saw the monogram of Jesus ablaze: the Greek chi and rho, the first two letters for the word *christ*; above the sign were the words "In this sign conquer."

There was more to come. The next night, Christ appeared to the general in a dream. The Lord of the Christians had apparently given his adopted commander an order. Constantine was to take the sign he had seen from heaven for his army's own symbol. This he did. After marking his own helmet, he ordered his men to do the same on their heads and shields. Maxentius's army met a standard never before seen among Rome's mighty legions. It was the sign of the Christian God. In a spectacular victory, Constantine's men crushed Maxentius outside of Rome at the Milvian Bridge; ten years later, Constantine would be sole ruler over the empire.

Constantine never forgot that dream. One of his first acts after the Battle of the Milvian Bridge was to lift the persecution that had been devouring Christians for the previous decade. Along with his co-emperor, Licinius, in AD 313, Constantine issued an unprecedented pronouncement from Milan. The text was recorded by his friend and collaborator Bishop Eusebius of Caesarea (d. 339) in what is the earliest comprehensive history of the Church: "As regards the Christians, in the previous letter sent to Your Dedication, definite instructions were issued regarding their places of assembly. We now further resolve that if any should appear to have bought these places either from our treasury or from any other source, they must restore them to these same Christians without payment or any demand for compensation and do so without negligence or hesitation."[4]

Not bad for a public apology. One can only imagine the political backlash Constantine would have endured.

---

4 Eusebius, *History of the Church*, trans. Paul L. Maier, 10.5.

Churches were to be restored, properties returned, freedom of worship granted to all.

Given recent imperial policy, the Edict of Milan was an unimaginable change of course. Christians had suffered brutal attacks. In a desperate attempt to restore unity, the recent emperor Diocletian (284–304) had sought to revive, as many before him had, a sense of loyalty and devotion to the imperial project. Unlike many, Diocletian was a good pagan in the sense that he was evidently sincere in his belief that the empire would crumble if Jupiter and the rest were not appeased. The presence of Christians obscured his vision of that future, so they were hunted. Eyewitnesses to these events have left graphic records. Under Diocletian, the Romans outdid themselves in their barbarities. First a decree went out that the church buildings should be leveled. Then the Scriptures were to be collected and burned. Some believers were simply crucified. Others were drowned, or decapitated, or burned to death, or beaten. In one corner of the empire, Christian women were tied by a foot and swung in the air, unclad, with their heads dragging across the ground. In another place, Christians were fastened to tree branches that had been bent by some sort of mechanical contraption and then soldiers "let the branches fly back to their natural position," tearing the victim's limbs in every direction.[5]

Understandably, Christians welcomed news of toleration as expressed in the edict as a divine miracle. Such a turn would have been as inconceivable for Roman Christians as was the fall of Communism to Eastern Europeans. And yet,

---

5 Ibid., 8.9.

more was to come. Victory at the Milvian Bridge set into motion a sequence of reversals that, outside of Providence, are difficult to interpret. Constantine's tolerance for the new Faith flowered and then blossomed into admiration.

~~~

Since that time, historians have wondered whether Constantine's conversion was genuine. That is no easy question. Some evidence suggests his turn was merely a matter of political expediency. Even after his conversion, he could be brutal. For example, there is the matter of the execution of his son and wife. The pagan historian Zosimus relates how Constantine had "killed his son, Crispus, on suspicion of having had intercourse with his step-mother, Fausta."[6] Constantine had recently passed legislation against adultery. His second wife, Fausta, claimed that her stepson, Crispus, had tried to seduce her. So the emperor put his son to death. Later, when Constantine discovered that the charge was fictitious and that it was Fausta who had acted the seducer, Constantine, in turn, had his servants lock Fausta in a steam bath until she suffocated.

Also recorded against his favor is the fact that he put off baptism till moments before his death. Less often remembered, though, is that such delays of ritual were common. The Church had been underground for three hundred years; much of her discipline had yet to be realized. Converts who were desirous of the Church's saving rites tended to put off baptism for prudential reasons. Baptism cleansed one thoroughly from sin and therefore granted to those who

---

6 Zosimus, *New History*, trans. R. T. Ridley, 2.29.
~~~

died shortly thereafter immediate entry to heaven. A rough warrior like Constantine traveled with memories he did not wish to carry into the next life. His example established a pattern that would help sanctify features of public life.

But in a way, none of this speculation matters. Whatever his private motivations, Constantine's public actions established precedents that would later be developed. In key respects, Constantine's legislation began to humanize the face of the empire and, through Rome's legacy, the politics of the West. Certainly, those Christians who knew him best, like the bishop Eusebius, thought Constantine's faith sincere. As Constantine had declared earlier to the bishops of the eastern empire: "I truly love, while I regard with reverence that power of which you have given abundant proofs, to the confirmation and increase of my faith. I hasten, then, to devote all my powers to the restoration of your most holy dwelling-place, which those profane and impious men have defiled by the contamination of violence."[7]

These words were not idle. Constantine built churches, many of them. He also used his immense power to reform the habits of the peoples that he ruled.

The first transformation was to limit the state's violence against the human person. Out of deference to Christ, Constantine reformed the penal system. Crucifixion was outlawed. It became illegal, for example, to confine prisoners to cells that left prisoners languishing in total darkness. In 315, he forbade the branding of the faces of prisoners. Such restraint may not seem particularly impressive to us eighteen centuries hence, but to the pagans and Christians of

---

7 Eusebius, *Life of Constantine*, trans. Ernest Cushing Richardson, 2.55.

the day, the custom of ritual human sacrifice was not a distant memory, and so such restraint appeared novel.[8] Also, features of Constantine's conduct in war were, by Roman standards, irregular. We are told, for one, that the Christian emperor tried "conscientiously to avoid any wanton sacrifice of human life." One way that he did this was by commanding his armies not to slaughter prisoners of war. This habit proved difficult to instill, and expensive. As his contemporary biographer relates:

> Accordingly he directed his victorious troops to spare the lives of their prisoners, admonishing them, as human beings, not to forget the claims of their common nature. And whenever he saw the passions of his soldiery excited beyond control, he repressed their fury by a largess of money, rewarding every man who saved the life of an enemy with a certain weight of gold. And the emperor's own sagacity led him to discover this inducement to spare human life, so that great numbers even of the barbarians were thus saved, and owed their lives to the emperor's gold.[9]

Other legislation encouraged respect for life in the family. He could show great concern for the poor.[10] Again, Romans had long used abortion and infanticide as secondary means of birth control. Constantine sought to end this. One of his laws provided money for the children of poor parents, thus partially undercutting one of the motives for killing. Divorce, too, he made difficult.

Pagan rulers prior to Constantine had, at times, shown great generosity toward their enemies and their own people. What made Constantine's legislation unique, and

---

8 Cf. Eusebius, *Oration in Praise of Constantine*, 13.7.

9 Eusebius, *Life of Constantine*, 2.13.

10 Ibid., 1.43.

precedent setting, was its new foundation. Man bears "the divine image." Mercy could no longer merely be left to the whim of the ruler but was a good due the human person because of man's divine origin. Theology had now infected the politics of the empire for the good. No doubt, Christian rulers after Constantine would sometimes fall grievously below this standard. But that a new standard had been raised, was clear.

~~~

The second legacy of Constantine's conversion in the West and the gift it imparted was the separation, or better, the beginning of a distinction between that which belongs to God and that which belongs to Caesar. By this I do not mean that Constantine set a template for a "wall of separation." Rather, in his legislation, he implicitly acknowledged that the duties of the state are not the highest duties, that the power of the state and its machinery does not command man's highest respect. The legislation I point to here was enacted on March 7, 321. On that day, he proclaimed Sunday a *civic* holiday. No public or legal business could be conducted on this day, save for work on farms.[11]

A small step, perhaps. But one that led to many others. From the point of view of both history and Catholic doctrine, Constantine's public recognition of the Sabbath is an early instance of the state's just cooperation with the Church. Since his enactment, Western nations have, until

---

11 For a list of some of Constantine's enlightened legislative acts, see Charles Herbermann, "Constantine the Great" in *Catholic Encyclopedia* (1908) and Hubert Jedin, ed., *History of the Church,* vol. 1 (London: Burns and Oats, 1980), 421–22.
~~~

recently regarded Sunday not only as a religious holiday but as a civic one too. Despite the advent of the big-box store and the birth of the 24/7 shopping cycle, the Church continues to side with her first emperor's view. In every country, Sundays should be set apart by the state. As the *Catechism of the Catholic Church* puts it, "In respecting religious liberty and the common good of all, Christians should seek the recognition of Sundays and the Church's holy days as legal holidays. They have to give everyone a public example of prayer, respect, and joy and defend their traditions as a precious contribution to the spiritual life of society" (CCC 2188).

The loss of Sunday as a secular holiday is one of the bleaker signs of our fall back into pagan politics, something out of which Constantine tried to pull his people. The Western legal tradition has had a long history since Constantine. But his religiously motivated civic service and his unwillingness to absorb all authority into the hands of the state set a precedent and example that would inspire other Christian rulers. It was a truth difficult to deny even if it was easy to ignore at times. An incident half a century after Constantine's death illustrates this difference.

Theodosius I (347–95) would be remembered as the last ruler to govern an undivided empire and the first emperor to officially outlaw paganism. The bishop St. Ambrose was his close advisor and a spiritual guide. In 390, a riot broke out in the city of Thessalonica, leaving several magistrates severely wounded or dead. In revenge for the disruption, the Christian ruler ordered a mass revenge killing. He set his soldiers loose, cutting down seven thousand people without trial. The attack on civilians was outrageous, to be sure, but not uncommon. What was without precedent is how the emperor responded to his bishop's rebuke.

Shortly after the event, Theodosius returned to Milan and attempted to enter the church. Ambrose was bishop. He blocked the emperor's path and delivered a memorable lesson in Christian statesmanship.

> You are a sovereign, Sir, of men of like nature with your own, and who are in truth your fellow slaves; for there is one Lord and Sovereign of mankind, Creator of the Universe. With what eyes then will you look on the temple of our common Lord—with what feet will you tread that holy threshold, how will you stretch forth your hands still dripping with the blood of unjust slaughter? How in such hands will you receive the all holy Body of the Lord?

The emperor did not enter. For eight months, Ambrose refused him entry into the church. When at last the emperor asked to be readmitted, for his penance, Ambrose made Theodosius sign an ingenious law. In the future, the state would observe a "waiting period" before an execution was delivered. An order for execution would stay for thirty days "that room might be made for the exercise of mercy and repentance."[12] Such delays remain in force even up to our own time. Finally, the bishop initiated a new liturgical custom. Theodosius was no longer allowed to sit with the clergy. Even though Theodosius was ruler, he was nevertheless a layman, a distinction that would have great political import. Over subsequent centuries, the West would continue to contemplate Jesus's admonition to give to Caesar what belongs to Caesar and to God what belongs to God. An ancient historian reflected on the docility of this head of state.

---

[12] Sozomen, *Ecclesiastical History*, trans. Chester D. Hartranft, 7.25.

"Educated as he had been in the sacred oracles, Theodosius knew clearly what belonged to priests and what to emperors. He therefore bowed to the rebuke of Ambrose, and retired sighing and weeping to the palace. After a considerable time, when eight months had passed away, the festival of our Savior's birth came round and the emperor sat in his palace shedding a storm of tears."[13]

~~~

Two final interventions of Constantine's were to leave an indelible mark on the trajectory of the West. One was the transfer of the imperial capital to the east; the other, the start of the great Council of Nicaea in the summer of AD 325, where the divinity of Christ was reaffirmed against the Arians.

Why did he move the capital? Though many among the poor of the empire had been attracted to the new Faith, the aristocracy remained largely pagan. Constantine had little desire to antagonize the Senate. Yet, as he saw the matter, the new Faith was to provide the glue needed to keep the old regime together. At Nicaea, Constantine had convened the world's bishops as a means of restoring some semblance of order to a community that had been hounded for decades. The chief doctrinal problem lay, of course, in answering Arius (c. 250–336). This renegade priest had sought to downgrade the stature of Christ from God to prophet. The bishops wanted orthodoxy. Constantine looked especially for unity. By convening the council, he lent the empire's sword and purse to give the Church room to make peace.

---

[13] Theodoret, *Ecclesiastical History*, trans. Blomfield Jackson, 5.17.
~~~

Though Constantine provided for two marvelous new churches in the ancient capital, Rome's associations with pagan cults would take centuries to efface. So he moved east. The situation of Constantinople, as it would be called, offered obvious military advantages. The city straddled both Europe and Asia; it commanded sea routes that could carry men and goods both east and west; it held natural fortifications on three sides; it could be filled with churches. After the council, the emperor returned to Rome as part of the celebrations marking the twentieth year of his reign. Once back in the old capital, he declined to partake in pagan ceremonies. Riots broke out and a statue depicting his person was defaced by a mob. St. John Chrysostom relates the emperor's prudent response. Instead of showing rage, he touched his face and, gently smiling, replied, "I am not able to see any wound inflicted on my face. Both the head and the face appear to be quite sound."[14]

Constantinople, or "New Rome," would from its birth be the world's first Christian capital. The city was consecrated 11 May 330 on the feast of the city's beloved martyr, Saint Mocius. Prior to its sack by the Muslims in 1458, some 325 male and female monasteries would find shelter within its embrace. The city would ensure that at least some of the goods of Greco-Roman civilization would project well into the second millennium of the Christian era. For that bulwark of civility we have much to be thankful. Long after Rome had fallen, long after the West had

---

[14] St. John Chrysostom, "On the Statues to the People of Antioch," trans. W. R. W. Stephens, in *A Select Library of the Nicene and Post-Nicene Fathers of the Christian Church*, ed. Philip Schaff, vol. 9, *Saint Chrysostom*, 21.11.

sunk beneath the waters of chaos, Constantine's imperial city preserved for civilization the science of the Greeks and the jurisprudence of the Romans. The Christian East would thus provide a constant reminder for the West of its past, even as old Rome began to forge its new future. To offer just one example, some of the classical texts lost to the West would resurface almost a thousand years later. Amid the persecution by Islam in the sixteenth century, groups of Byzantine Christians fled to the West, and so breathed new life into the energies of the emerging Italian Renaissance. Among these refugees was the erudite Cardinal Bessarion (1403–1472). In 1468, the cardinal bequeathed to the senate of Venice some 482 Greek and 264 Latin manuscripts.[15] The eighteenth-century historian Edward Gibbon paid tribute to the contribution of these exiles in these words: "The restoration of the Greek letters in Italy was prosecuted by a series of emigrants who were destitute of fortune and endowed with learning, or at least with language. From the terror or oppression of the Turkish arms, the natives of Thessalonica and Constantinople escaped to a land of freedom, curiosity and wealth."[16]

But long before Italy could be a land of "freedom, curiosity, and wealth," it had to suffer through the trials of war, hunger, and plague, and learn again the lessons of peace from the monks who sought quiet.

---

15 For a study on the migration of Greek texts to the West, see Niels Gaul, "The Manuscript Tradition," in *A Companion to the Ancient Greek Language*, ed. E. Bakker (London: Blackwell Publishing, 2010), 81.

16 Edward Gibbon, *The History of the Decline and Fall of the Roman Empire*, ed. J. B. Bury (London: Metheun and Co., 1902), 7:123.

4

MONKS: THE GIFT OF STABILITY

"We ought, therefore, to establish a school for the Lord's service."

Benedict of Nursia

IF you would be perfect, sell what you possess "and come, follow me" (Mt 19:21). Such is the charter of the monk. The word comes from the Greek *monos*, which means "alone." One of the marvelous ironies of history is that those in the Church who have fled the world have very often done the most to save it and that those who have left the bustle of the cities have sometimes done the most to encourage civility. This describes well the gift of Benedict and his children.

Born of an aristocratic family, Benedict was sent early to Rome that he might receive an education in the classical liberal arts. He did not finish that education. Instead, the young man left the ancient city to seek another kind of learning. Near the opening of Benedict's ancient biography, Pope Gregory the Great (r. 540–604), his former pupil, recounts the young man's decision to leave Rome with these words:

> He was born in the district of Norcia of distinguished parents, who sent him to Rome for a liberal education. But when he

> saw many of his fellow students falling headlong into vice, he stepped back from the threshold of the world in which he had just set foot. For he was afraid that if he acquired any of its learning he, too, would later plunge, body and soul, into the dread abyss. In his desire to please God alone, he turned his back on further studies, gave up home and inheritance and resolved to embrace the religious life.[1]

Shortly after this flight, Benedict settled in a cave in the hills outside Subiaco, some forty miles east of Rome. He was not yet twenty. It was during these three years of silence, as Pope Pius XII would reflect fourteen centuries later, that the youth laid "those solid foundations of Christian perfection on which he was given later to raise a mighty building of lofty heights."[2] As with every true reformer, before he could aid others, Benedict first needed to master himself.

There is nothing uncommon in the experience. How often it is that when the mind is at rest, the imagination will erupt, carrying the affections down some unholy current of desire. So it was for this youth. In Rome, Benedict met many exiting and attractive people from his own class, including eligible young women. One day, while he was alone in his cave, the figure of a woman refashioned itself before his mind's eye. That fantasy enflamed desire. Passion threatened to overthrow his will. So agitated was his imagination that he nearly picked up and fled. Who knows what would have become of the West had Benedict decided that day to run into the arms of a woman? In any case, he

---

1 Gregory the Great, *Dialogues*, trans. Odo John Zimmerman, opening of book 2.

2 Pius XII, *Fulgens Radiatur* (1947), 8.

never left his cave. And, in a moment of fiery repentance, the youth looked wildly about him for some means by which to prove his manly resolve. He found it in a nearby patch of thorns. Tearing off his clothes, he threw himself into the bush, twisting his limbs again and again across the sharp nails of this unlikely mistress. Gregory concludes this episode with characteristic Roman reserve, saying of the young monk that he "never experienced another temptation of this kind."[3]

Soon after this first conquest, local people began to seek his advice. A group of monks even asked him to serve as their abbot. Benedict reluctantly agreed. The monks, however, grew exasperated with his discipline. They eventually determined to poison him. During a meal one evening, as Benedict raised his hand in benediction over a jug of wine, which his murderous brethren had hoped would soon touch his lips, an invisible stone was hurtled across the room. Nobody saw the rock. But Gregory relates that the clay exploded in their midst as though a hand had thrown a projectile; his life was spared. Benedict returned to his own solitude, where he would have time to reconsider the ways of men. During this next, creative period of his formation, he would weigh his own experiments in human development against the failures and successes of others, one man in particular.

~~~

Monasticism by Benedict's time had existed in an experimental mode for some two hundred years. Although

---

3 Gregory, *Dialogues,* 2.2.
~~~

Benedict would frame the lasting house, and his sons perpetuate the gift of stability to hundreds of self-sustaining communities of prayer and study and work, its foundations were laid by others. Bishop-theologians of the fourth century, like Athanasius and Augustine and Basil, did much to articulate the doctrine that would support the spirituality of the monks, but more than these, everyone since even before Benedict has looked to the Church's first hero of the spiritual life, Antony. The long life of Antony of Egypt (c. 251–356) straddled the last hours of imperial persecution and first moments of imperial patronage. His life painted the essential background to the great drama in which Benedict and his rule would later take the lead part.

Like Benedict, much of what we know of Antony comes from the pen of another saint, the beleaguered and oft-exiled bishop Athanasius of Alexandria. Athanasius published *The Life of Antony* just after the saint's death, and it was an instant best seller. Antony had already become the subject of considerable rumor. The outlines of his life were familiar to many: the sale of his inheritance, the apprenticeship under other holy men by age twenty, the two decades in near solitude, and the last long years of prayer intermittently interrupted by pilgrims, clerics, and even the emperor, all seeking the miracle worker's advice and favor. What Athanasius most wished to impress upon his readers, however, was not the splendor of Antony's miracles but rather the miracle of Antony's discipline. The word Athanasius uses to describe Antony's discipline is *askesis*. For this term, there is no easy translation. Originally it refers to the practices of an athlete, and then is transferred to the "practice," the "discipline," or more generally, the "way of life" of the martyrs.[4] What this sort of discipline produces is the gift of a unified self. Through Antony's example, patterns for the monastic life of the subsequent centuries would be set. Thus the monk is a man who works with his hands (in Antony's case, weaving baskets); he endures long fasts; his day is absorbed in Scripture; he becomes skilled in the discernment of spirits, even to the point of casting out devils. If we consider the monk a soldier for Christ, we see in Antony's *Life* a contest waged on two fronts: the battle against devils and the battle against the self.

The devil's attacks against Antony, though real, became the occasion of overcoming the restless ego. Athanasius's biography relates how, early on in his new life, Antony had shown such growth in virtue that he was loved by all who knew him. It was at this point that the devil unleashed his wrath in the form of bewildering temptations. The devil's first attack is directed toward Antony's sympathy. Antony worries for his sister's care, then his family's estate, and then at his own ability to endure. "In short," the devil causes "the greatest confusion in Antony's thoughts." Athanasius continues:

> First [the devil] tried to unsettle him at night by means of hostile hordes and terrifying sounds, and then he attacked him by day with weapons that were so obviously his that no one could doubt that it was against the devil that Antony was fighting. For the devil tried to implant dirty thoughts but Antony pushed them away by constant prayer. . . . At night the devil would turn himself into the attractive form of a beautiful

---

4 For references see Walter Bauer, *A Greek–English Lexicon of the New Testament and Other Early Christian Literature*, trans. William F. Arndt and F. Wilbur Gingrich (Chicago: University of Chicago Press, 1952).

> woman, omitting no detail that might provoke lascivious thoughts, but Antony called to mind the fiery punishment of hell and the torment inflicted by worms: in this way he resisted the onslaught of lust.

Having no success, the evil spirit changed tactics. In his bid to overthrow the man of God, he turns from the inciting of pleasures to the inflicting of pains. At this time, Antony dwells alone in the desert in a cave. But the devil was afraid, Athanasius relates, that Antony "might cause the desert to become inhabited" by other seekers of Christ.

~~~

Athanasius's book won a wide audience. Men such as Augustine would be moved by Antony's example, as he recounts in his own *Confessions*.[5] Athanasius, the Church's lead defender against Arius and the powerful nobility that supported the heresiarch, knew that Christ's flock could not ultimately depend upon the patronage of kings and courts. The Christian revolution was first a matter of the spirit. Schools, economies, and laws would all have to be transformed; every exterior conquest of the Faith, he knew, was but the result of a far more difficult conquest: that of the self. Athanasius makes the lesson clear in his final paragraph of his *Life*: "Read this book carefully to the brothers," he exhorts, so that all may know that Christ grants fame to those who lead "a life of withdrawal in remote mountain places." Athanasius refers principally, of course, to other would-be monks. But these "mountain places" can signify more than literal places; more importantly, the true

5 See Augustine, *Confessions*, 8.14.
~~~

imitators of Antony, he seems to suggest, are those who seek the lofty kingdom that is first *within*. Athanasius, as a bishop suffering continual and repeated persecution at the hands of Christian emperors, understood well the dynamics of the Church's coming political entanglements.

No one could say that the conversion of empire had not brought blessings—the freedom to convene councils, public grants of land, new churches. State patronage had brought to the Church honor and wealth. Over the subsequent decades, however, into her company would stream men and women who looked to her rites for more than the blessings of heaven. In the years between Antony and Benedict, it became popular to be Christian. Zealous men fled in such numbers after Antony that the desert of Egypt became as a city. And here is the point: the monks prior to Benedict sought a return to combat conditions. If the world could no longer provide these conditions, adventurous men and women determined to find them elsewhere: in the interior struggle of the passions of the soul. Monks after the pattern of Antony became "living martyrs."

Thus, in a marvelous way during the fourth and fifth centuries, the Church gave birth to a new kind of hero: a hero of the spirit. Prehistoric Greece, whose voice sings in Homer's *Iliad*, esteemed the warrior; Plato's *Republic* idealized the philosopher; Cicero's *On Duties* celebrated the statesmen. To this list, the Church added her own contribution: the saint. Male or female, young or old, the saint's deeds depend upon neither wealth nor class (one of the early popes, St. Callistus, had been a slave) nor arms nor learning nor even clerical status but merely that most difficult thing of all: the will to love God. To enact this ideal was the aim of the monk. As one of the other pre-Benedictine fathers of monasticism, John Cassian, explained to an early seeker: "The end of our profession, as we have said, is the kingdom of God or the kingdom of heaven; but the goal or *scopos* is purity of heart."[6] One man above all others would provide the vehicle through which the revolution in the hearts of individual Christians would transform a continent and the world. That man was named Benedict.

Drawing upon the Egyptian monastic experience, Benedict could survey the results. No doubt, as with the case of St. Antony, God could raise up singular individuals. Benedict's own conclusions, though, were tempered by his Roman instinct. Good men want conversion. Taming the heart requires a method. The excessive independence of the hermits, as much as the chaotic freedom of what he terms the wandering monks or "gyrovagues" (*gyro*, "circle," and *vagus*, "straying," "vague"), needed to be wrestled into a replicable pattern of life and an enduring gift for future generations. This Benedict set out to offer. He would soon gain the chance to test his ideas. A group of men once again gathered around Benedict, now in Subiaco, sixty miles east of St. Peter's in Rome. It was here that Benedict set down his thoughts for good order and stability in his *Rule*.

~~~

What is most remarkable about St. Benedict's *Rule* is its moderation. Fidelity to godly habit will be the means to salvation. What the rule offers to men is a new kind of education. From its preface: "We ought, therefore, to establish

---

6 John Cassian, *The Conferences*, trans. B. Ramsey, 1.4.3.
~~~

a school for the Lord's service." Benedict meant to, literally. The Latin term for school (*schola*) is the same that would be applied to the place where boys and girls learned to count and read. Except this school would be directed toward holiness. And though the school might be strict, he declares at the outset that he hopes to establish *nihil asperum, nihil grave*, "nothing rough, nothing burdensome."

Prayer is the central work of Benedict's monk. Time must also be devoted to manual labor. Together these two activities would come to be ordered around the seven offices, the *Opus Dei*, or "work of God." Roughly 10 percent of the rule is devoted explicitly to explaining the community's method of prayer. Which psalms to pray, in what order, during which seasons, is woven into the constitution of his school. In the *Rule*, he cites the Psalms as his immediate authority. "Seven times a day I praise you" (Ps 119:164). And so shall the monks. Of course, here too, Benedict was building upon past customs. Early on, Jewish practice had begun to evolve into a new Christian discipline. On the prayer of the late evening (which Benedict calls Matins, said about 2 a.m.), around the year AD 200, Hippolytus, another early Christian writer, counsels: "About midnight, get out of your bed and wash and pray." The same writer continues, "It is very important that we pray at least once every hour; for the ancients have handed this practice down to us and taught us that this is how we are to keep watch."[7]

St. Paul had said that we should "pray constantly" (1 Thes 5:17). But even energetic men need footholds if they

7 Hippolytus, *Apostolic Tradition*, in *The Roman Breviary*, bilingual edition (1963), 1:5.

are to mount a cliff. Benedict's method supplied the pegs. After citing Psalm 119, Benedict adds his own gloss: "We will fulfill this sacred sevenfold number if we perform the duties of our service at the time of Morning Prayer, Prime, Tierce, Sext, None, Vespers, and Compline."[8] Such was born the canonical hours—what would become for all Christendom the designated times of communal prayer. Over the course of centuries, each hour would come to take on a specific character, which we can schematize.[9]

Matins (2 a.m., night)	Second Coming of Christ
Lauds (5 a.m., early morning)	Praise for spiritual resurrection
Prime (6 a.m., first light)	Preparation for the day's work
Terce (9 a.m., third hour)	Invocation of the Holy Spirit
Sext (12 noon, midday)	Prayer for deliverance from sin
None (3 p.m., ninth hour)	Prayer for perseverance
Vespers (6 p.m., sunset)	Thanksgiving for blessings
Compline (end of the day)	Act of contrition

If life is a pilgrimage, these are the moments during which the true seeker can find refreshment. In the pagan imagination, nothing new really happened. Empires might rise and fall to form the backdrop of a man's birth and death, but the patterns of history were like the tides of the sea: unremitting. Not so for Benedict's sons. Every life is a drama, and all acts are played on the stage of a divinely ordered comedy. Thus the need for vigilance. Across these few years of travel, each man can either arrive at his final true home or not. By binding himself to a predictable

8 Benedict, *Rule*, trans. Fahey, ch. 16.

9 I draw on Parsch in his commentary at the head of *The Roman Breviary* (1963), 1:3–12.

pattern of feasts and prayers, the monk attains the freedom to make of his will a sacrifice of praise. Spiritual freedom within consecrated stability is the aim and gift of Benedict's ordering of time.

~~~

On Benedict's model, holiness would be sought and found through the ordinary tasks of a believer's life. This aspiration will find expression elsewhere in the Catholic tradition, as in the spiritual counsels of St. Francis de Sales (1567–1622) or, in our own time, St. Josemariá Escrivá's dynamic movement *Opus Dei*. But it began with Benedict. The whole day, from morning till evening, is marked by a sober moderation, with time enough for rest as well as exertion, common prayer, and silence. Plato's ideal scholar was a man of leisure who concentrated almost solely on intellectual affairs. Not so for Benedict. In imitation of Christ and the Apostles, when Benedict's sons work with their hands, as the *Rule* says in its forty-eighth chapter—*tunc vere manachi sunt—then* truly they are monks. We see here how the principle of the incarnation modified the old classical ideal of learning. The results were stunning.

Besides teaching the West how to order time under the light of eternity, I mention two final gifts that Benedict's sons and daughters bequeathed: advanced agriculture and devoted scholarship. Benedictines became masters of fruitful husbandry. They were, we might say, the West's first true environmentalists.[10] Wherever his monks settled, they rendered the surrounding landscape beautiful. They literally

---

10 See Pope Francis's reflections on St. Benedict's approach to work in *Laudato Si* (2015), 126.
~~~

founded the modern science of agriculture. To take one example, in the seventh century, the Benedictine's planted themselves near the south coast of England, in Southampton, in what was then a vast, deserted, swampland. After centuries of the Benedictine's care, an eyewitness in the twelfth century could describe that same swampland as a vision of paradise:

> Not an inch of land as far as the eye can reach lies uncultivated. Here the soil is hidden by fruit trees; there by vines stretched upon the ground or trailed on trellises. Nature and art rival each other, the one supplying all that the other forgets to produce. O deep and pleasant solitude! Thou hast been given by God to the monks so that their mortal life may daily bring them nearer to heaven.[11]

Benedictines also guarded the old books. In 410, Rome had been sacked. It would fall again in 476 when Odoacer deposed the last Western emperor. While illiterate men fought over the spoils of Rome's dying civilization, monks copied and stored scrolls away for better times. It was a long wait. Literacy in those centuries was rare. To give some sense of the learning of the time, the relatively enlightened king Theodoric, ruler of the Ostrogoths and all Italy from AD 493–526, could neither read nor write. The texts of Homer, Thucydides, Sophocles, and Cicero would have little value for such a warrior, and so the monks of prayer stored them away until the time that the men of war would grow impatient with fighting and look again to the arts and sciences of peace.

---

[11] This description is from the medieval English historian William of Malmesbury and cited in Thomas Woods, *How the Catholic Church Built Western Civilization* (Washington, D.C.: Regnery Publishing, 2005), 31.

But the monks did not simply copy and store books. Even more than preserving texts, Benedict's *Rule* gave men a reason once more for wanting to take them up again, and write new ones. Indeed, they not only preserved knowledge of the liberal arts; they also began the long work of ennobling them and disseminating their benefits.

In 597, Pope Gregory the Great, Benedict's original biographer, sent a small party of monks, a traveling outpost of civilization, from Rome to the frontiers of England. Their mission was to preach to the pagan Angle and Saxon tribes that reigned where Caesar's armies once marched. The party's leader was Augustine of Canterbury. He brought with him a copy of the *Rule*. The men continued the monastic traditions they had learned in Rome, sharing in a communal life, and singing the psalter.[12] As Augustine and his men traveled up and down the English coast, they preached Christ and handed on the *Rule*. The movement spread. Even the Celtic monks, after a protracted battle, came to adopt the Roman discipline, which they themselves would pass along to others. By the eighth century, the British Isles were sending their own missionaries and books back to the continent. One of these international ambassadors of a newly burgeoning Christian culture was Boniface (680–755), born in Devonshire and soon to be dubbed apostle to the Germans. Another was Bede (673–735), the first historian of the English people. Yet another missionary monk trained in the school of Benedict was Alcuin (735–804), who was from York and the greatest scholar of his age. When Charlemagne began his own work of civilizational reconstruction, he summoned Alcuin to his capital in 782.

12 See Bede, *Ecclesiastic History*, 1.27.

There the monk would lead a group of scholars to head up a court school and chart an educational program that would lay the foundations for the first great European renaissance that was to come in the twelfth century.

It is true that three centuries after Theodoric, Charlemagne, in AD 800, the year he was crowned emperor of the Holy Roman Empire, could still neither read nor write. Yet, unlike Theodoric, Christendom's new ruler knew better the value of learning. Generations of monastic labors had begun to bear rich fruit. Charlemagne could speak Latin and Greek and loved to have St. Augustine's *City of God* read to him during his evening meal.[13] After a long night of political disorder, the silver streaks of dawn had appeared. And it was chiefly due to the labors of a dozen generations of Benedictines that the light broke through. Soon that light would grow and, with it, the spread of learning throughout all of Christendom. Like Abraham in the household of faith, St. Benedict can well be called the Patriarch of Western culture.

At its height, the Benedictine family could claim some 37,000 houses, and among their sons and daughters some 30 popes, 46 kings, 51 queens, and 1,600 archbishops.[14] The monks taught the West a stable method of prayer, how

---

13 See Einhard, *The Life of Charlemagne*, 24–25.

14 Figures cited by Cardinal Newman in *Historical Sketches*, vol. 2, "The Mission of St. Benedict" (London: Longmans, Green, and Co., 1906), 372. As of the most recent statistics, printed in the *Catalogus Monasteriorum O.S.B.* (Romae: SS. Patriarchae Benedicti Familiae Confoederatae, 2010), p.489, some 7,000 monks belong world-wide to the fully professed family of Benedictines. (My thanks to Fr. James at St. Benedict Abbey, Still River, MA, for these figures.)

to join science with service, and cultivated the literal and figurative wilderness of Europe's soil. It was these habits of mind that made possible the birth of a future Christian civilization, to whose first fruits we turn next.

5

SCHOLARS: THE GIFT OF THE UNIVERSITIES

"Lanterns shining in the house of God . . ."

Pope Alexander IV

LONG after Gregory the Great turned Attila the Hun out of Rome, the strong arms of Alfred and Charlemagne established order among Christians, and the preaching of Cyril and Methodius gave a new alphabet to the Slavs—not so long after the monks at Cluny had reformed discipline among the clergy, and during the days that St. Francis wandered Italy and Richard the Lion hearted fought Saladin in the east—the first glories of this new civilization were rising up along the Seine river, and along the Thames, in the towering Cathedrals, and in their schools. Europe had finally recovered. Under the tutelage of the Church, a novel political and social reality appeared in Europe that would, in time, rival and surpass the legacy of pagan Rome: Christendom. It was as though the champagne bottle had been shaken just enough; a new energy, a new devotion, and a new intelligence burst forth across the territories of this new civilization.

"Lanterns shining in the house of God"—that was the name Pope Alexander IV (r. 1254–61) gave to the universities.[1] Through these institutions, the Church offered to the world its first truly international and secular NGO (non-governmental organization), its first experience of legally protected intellectual freedom, and a set of rigorous methods for testing hypotheses. The first universities established themselves at Paris, Oxford, and Bologna. The University of Paris, whose charter dates from 1200, itself grew out of two earlier Catholic institutions: the Cathedral school housed at Notre Dame and the house of studies run by the monks at St. Genevieve Abbey, also in Paris. Early universities had no buildings of their own. What defined the institution was its essential activity: teaching and learning. In Paris, as in Oxford, professors rented spots in a church, and students would pay locals for a room with a bed.

The term *university* today typically points to the universality of subjects taught. Something of this is true of the medieval universities as well. More precisely, though, it was the international character of the student body and its professors that set it apart from a merely local or national school. A master who graduated from Bologna, for instance, was granted the authority to teach, in principle, anywhere within Christendom. Armed with their learning, scholars and students traveled extensively. Thus, though Thomas Aquinas (1225–74) grew up in Italy, he met his finest teacher, the German-born Albertus Magnus, in Paris, and to take an example from the north, the intellectual leader of the next century, John Duns Scotus, was a

---

1 See H. Daniel-Rops, *Cathedral and Crusade: Studies of the Medieval Church 1050-1350*, trans. John Warrington (London: J. M. Dent and Sons, 1957), 311.

Scotsman who traveled between Oxford and Paris, and was buried in Cologne.

From the beginning, the universities jealously guarded their independence from local interference. Conflict between "townies" and "gownies" not infrequently arose. In 1204, to take one instance, a riot broke out between members of the university scholars of Oxford and the people of the city. All teaching shut down. Some scholars fled (that's how Cambridge got started); others appealed to the pope. Classes resumed in 1209, but this time on a more solid footing. Oxford had armed herself with a papal charter. Against the wishes of city officials, scholars were given authority over students and professors. A chancellor was appointed. The city of Oxford was ordered to reduce fees for student-renters to half the price of the market value and pay the university an annual sum for damages—a custom that ended only in 1923.

This brings us to the Church's first remarkable gift to the medieval university, a gift whose benefits would ennoble the West's developing intellectual tradition for centuries: the gift of academic freedom. This privilege was, in many instances, guaranteed literally by the pope. Prior to the Reformation, European Catholics had founded eighty-one universities. Thirty-three of these had a papal charter as their founding legal document; twenty universities had both a papal and an imperial (or royal) charter; the rest had either imperial or royal charters, or no charters.[2] Later historians have sometimes located the origin of academic freedom in the eighteenth-century Enlightenment. That is incorrect.

---

2 See Edward Pace, "Universities" in *The Catholic Encyclopedia* (1912).

The first mention of the term comes from a papal document of 1220. The context was as follows. City officials at Bologna were demanding that university members take an oath of allegiance to the city. The scholars baulked. In order to retain their independence, and their fellowship as an international community of scholars, they appealed to the one supranational authority that they thought could take effective action: Rome. Pope Honorius III himself encouraged the young community to maintain its autonomy against the city; against any and all challengers, the university, he said, ought to defend its "scholastic freedom" (*libertas scholastica*)—and it did, with the papacy's aid.[3]

All across Europe, these fledgling communities looked to the bishop of Rome. The University of Toulouse was an early university established under the authority of a pope, in this case Gregory IX. As at Oxford, lectures at Paris had been suspended due to a conflict between scholars and town officials, and in 1229, the university itself dissolved. The new foundation at Toulouse saw a marketing opportunity. After the fallout in Paris, the upstart institution ran an advertisement to attract new members with a circulated letter. The upstart boasted money and safety from "the raging mob" of townies. Under the patronage of the pope, and with the cooperation of a compliant count, security and intellectual liberty were offered to all. Members of the university were promised access to "the books of Aristotle which were forbidden at Paris." These scholars taunted: "What then will you lack? Scholastic liberty? By no means,

3 See William J. Hoye's classic study "The Religious Roots of Academic Freedom" in *Theological Studies* 58 (1997): 409–28.

since here you can enjoy your own liberty tied to no one's apron strings."[4] Between the twelfth and eighteenth centuries, the universities of Europe enjoyed fantastic wealth under the patronage of Church and State, and the almost uninterrupted intellectual freedom to pursue knowledge of everything from metaphysics to mechanics. Hundreds of students labored in the cloistered colleges of Oxford, some ten thousand attended at Bologna; at one time, it is said, Paris cradled as many students as inhabitants; the city remained a center of Catholic intellectual life until leaders of the French Revolution closed the university in 1792.

At this juncture, let us address a persistent prejudice. Didn't the Church censure academics? Hasn't science been at war with religion? And by the way, what about Galileo?

~~~

It is still not uncommon to find in popular histories of science biased or ignorant accounts of the Church's condemnation of Galileo Galilei, written as though the late medieval Church had been, in principle, opposed to experimental methods of observation. Such books may sell well as science fiction. They offer little by way of credible history. The incident was unfortunate, no doubt. And in 1992, John Paul II attempted to make amends, as we'll see. But in this case, the exception proves the rule. It is the only obvious example of such a blunder on the side of the Church in a long and glorious love affair.

---

4 "A Letter from the Masters of Toulouse to the Other Universities" (1229), in *University Records and Life in the Middle Ages*, ed. Lynn Thorndike (New York: Columbia University Press, 1944), 34–35.
~~~

Those who use Galileo's condemnation to pit the Church against science must gloss over overwhelming evidence, among which I list the following. First, Catholics had always been leading patrons of education. The birth of the universities in the Middle Ages is an obvious instance of this. But even more, the Church's early development of catechetical schools, its absorption by the fourth century of the most sophisticated traditions of Greek and Roman philosophy, her preservation of literary and scientific works, her monastic and cathedral schools, her education of orphans, the Benedictine's advancement of the experiential sciences, and, long before Galileo, the Jesuits' devotion to astronomy, finds no parallel, anywhere.[5] Second, priests and religious have always been well represented among the sciences. In one nineteenth-century catalogue of empirical scientists, about 10 percent, or 862 out of 8,847, were members of the Catholic clergy.[6] Third, Catholic clergy have not only modeled the compatibility of theological and empirical study, they have often excelled as leaders in original

---

5 The literature tracking this involvement is legion. A compendious overview treating Catholic investment in education up to the early twentieth century may be found in the entry "Schools" by Perrier and Maher et al. in *The Catholic Encyclopedia* (1912). Christopher Dawson's *The Crisis of Western Education* (Washington, D.C.: Catholic University of America Press, 2010) provides a magisterial narrative. For a survey of contemporary parochial education in North America see Ryan Topping, *The Case for Catholic Education* (Kettering, OH: Angelico Press, 2015).

6 The multivolume study is called *Biographisch-Literarisches Handwörterbuch* (Leipzig, 1863), cited in J. Hagen, "Science and the Church" in *The Catholic Encyclopedia* (1912).

scientific research, in some cases serving as founders of their field.

A merely passing familiarity with the biographies of the pioneers of science should give the Church's critics pause. To name a few, one might point to the Franciscan Roger Bacon (d. 1294), early proponent of the experimental method and among the first to study optics; Cardinal Nicholas of Cusa (d. 1446), possibly the first to have discovered the benefit of concave lenses to the treatment of myopia (shortsightedness); Nicolaus Copernicus (d. 1543), who nearly a century before Galileo proposed that the earth orbits the sun; Athanasius Kircher, S. J. (d. 1680), a polymath linguist and early decipherer of hieroglyphics who, on the side, developed one of the first counting machines; Blessed Nicholas Stenu (d.1 686) is named among the founders of geology; Giuseppe Piazzi (d. 1826) discovered the first known asteroid or minor planet, Ceres; the Benedictine father Gregory Mendel (d. 1884) was also the father of modern genetics; closer to our own day, Georges Lemaître (d. 1966) ranks along with Albert Einstein among the most renowned twentieth-century physicists for his development of the Big Bang theory.[7] And this is not even to mention the contributions of lay Catholics such as the mathematician Blaise Pascal (d. 1662), chemist Louis Pasteur (d. 1895), or pioneering physicians like St. Giuseppe Moscati (d. 1927)

---

7 One can start with Wikipedia, then go to Holden and Pinsent's *The Catholic Gift to Civilization* (London: Catholic Truth Society, 2011), then to Wood, *How the Catholic Church Built Western Civilization*, and A. G. Crombie's *Medieval and Early Modern Science,* 2 vols. (New York: Doubleday, 1959).

and John Billings (d. 2007), leaders in the application of insulin and in the tracking of human fertility.

But let us return to Galileo Galilei. Galileo himself did not regard scientific inquiry to be in conflict with his Catholic faith. Galileo was a believing Catholic and included among his friends the future Pope Urban VIII, pontiff at the time of his condemnation. In his own writings, Galileo passionately argued for the harmony of faith and reason. His manifesto on the subject, which is also one of the most important documents in the history of science, was circulated under the form of a public letter to Christine de Lorraine (1615). The text is punctuated with quotations from St. Augustine, as when he recommends: "It is to be held an unquestionable truth that whatever the sages of this world have demonstrated concerning physical matters is in no way contrary to our Bibles; hence whatever the sages teach in their books that is contrary to the holy Scriptures may be concluded without any hesitation as false."[8]

We have no evidence that Galileo's faith in the harmony of science and Catholic belief was anything but sincere. As well as having personal friendships and collaborators among many of the leading clergy of his time, he entrusted the education of his daughters to a convent, one of whom later took the name of Sister Maria Celeste.

So whence arose the conflict? This is a story that has been treated many times. A thorough evaluation would pull us through the personalities, politics, and religious factions of the day, but from the side of the Church, the

---

8 Drake's translation of Galileo's letter in *Discoveries and Opinions of Galileo* (New York: Doubleday, 1957), 194. Galileo here is quoting from St. Augustine's *De Genesi ad literam*, 1.21.

chief difficulty with Galileo's position was as follows.[9] He trumpeted a view of a Sun-centered solar system before he had established overwhelming empirical evidence, and this model conflicted with certain established interpretations of scriptural passages. Recall that the priest-scientist Nicholas Copernicus had long before posited the same conclusion. Until conclusive evidence could be shown, however, members on the Church's tribunal refused to accept heliocentrism as *more* than a hypothesis. Pope Urban III was himself a patron of Galileo, and even encouraged the scientist's work until Galileo deliberately snubbed the pontiff by breaking their gentlemen's agreement: the pope, indeed, had no problem with Galileo continuing to build his case, so long as he, in the meantime, did not insist that the science was settled. By no means was the science settled. At the time, and for centuries after, it was far from clear that Galileo was in the right. As astronomers recognized, if the earth truly is in motion, then we should be able to observe an apparent change in the position of stars. The name for this apparent change is called stellar parallax—something only definitively observed some two centuries later, in 1838, by the German astronomer Friedrich Bessel.

Church authorities had another reason to be reluctant. Besides offering a theory that would overturn centuries of previous observation, Galileo's work challenged doctrine, or what was perceived by many to be settled doctrine. It seemed in particular to contradict a common interpretation of parts of Scripture. Joshua 10:11–13, for one, suggested

---

9 Two helpful treatments can be found in Wood, *How the Catholic Church Built Western Civilization*, pp. 67–74, and Stillman Drake's *Galileo* (New York: Hill and Wang, 1980).

that the earth, not the sun, lay at the center of the world. In the end, and unfortunately, Galileo was adamant that the theologians should accept his theory as more than such, and he refused to treat the Copernican model as a hypothesis, against the express wish of his old friend Urban III. After leaving the door open for Galileo to pursue his work essentially unhindered, and then having it slammed in their face, the ecclesial tribunal that was responsible for evaluating Galileo's work was placed in an awkward position. The scientist's works were put on the index of prohibited books. And Galileo, unfortunately, lived out his last years under house arrest first, we might add, as a guest of the archbishop of Siena and then in his own villa.

In evaluating the Church's regrettable response, another extenuating factor needs to be taken into account. Beyond the personalities involved, Galileo's birth came about twenty years after the Council of Trent and the first shock of the Protestant Reformation. One of the criticisms Reformers tossed at the Church was that she no longer anchored doctrine to Scripture. Catholics too quickly took flight, it was argued, in allegorical interpretations. And there is some truth to this. Since at least the time of Origen in the third century, Catholics had utilized both literal and allegorical methods. The *Song of Songs* in particular was a favorite among allegorizing exegetes, a Jewish story about lovers that became a tale of Christ and the soul, or Christ and his mystical bride. Origen himself produced a ten-volume commentary on the book; in the twelfth century, Bernard of Clairvaux preached eighty-six sermons on the *Song of Songs*; it is the last book upon which Thomas Aquinas lectured as he lay dying. From the era of the Fathers on, a Psalm was far more likely to interest exegetes for how it illumined the soul's affection for Jesus than for what it revealed about David's Semitic influences.[10] These impulses are good and right, and yet, at times some truths need to be emphasized more than others. And in Galileo's time, what needed defense was the literal sense of Scripture. Protestants claimed to derive their authority from Scripture. Catholics, likewise, claimed the Bible as God's Word. In the midst of the religious politics of the day, upholding the *literal* interpretation of Scripture—against Galileo—was seen by leaders in the Church as necessary to making good that claim.

It was unfortunate that the rise of the scientific method emerged at the very moment the Church felt her back up against a wall. All at once two potentially rival systems made claims to Catholic Europe's intellectual allegiance. On the one side, vied Protestants. On the other, pressed an emerging method and body of scientific observations. Both sides threatened to crash against literal interpretations of Scripture. Galileo was intent on pressing the conflict. He wanted theologians to clarify more sharply the bounds between the study of the God who made the heavens and the heavens that God made. Galileo was a man of indefatigable self-confidence. "If Scripture cannot err," Galileo wrote to Benedetto Castelli, his Benedictine student, "certain of its interpreters and commentators can and do so in many ways."[11]

---

10 For background, see J. Paul Tanner, "The History of Interpretation of the Song of Songs," in *Bibliotheca Sacra* 154: 613 (1997): 23–46.

11 Galileo *Letter* of 21 November 1613, in *Edizione nazionale delle Opere di Galileo Galilei,* dir. A. Favaro, edition of 1968, vol. V, p.

A scene likely drawn from the Sumerian *Epic of Gilgamesh*, over a millennium older than either Homer of the Bible, the tale testifies to man's persistent desire for immortality—a desire only satisfied, so the early Christians proclaimed, through baptism in Christ.

The Christian poet Dante Alighieri in his *Divine Comedy* honors Virgil for his service in pointing Gentiles to expect a world savior.

The Roman Emperor Nero torching Christians. What the early Christian martyrs bequeathed to the West was a model of personal sacrifice for the sake of truth.

Constantine at the Battle of the Milvian Bridge (painting by Giulio Romano, 1520-24). Through Constantine's legacy, the Church gave the West two enduring gifts: a pattern of religiously motivated secular service and the principled distinction between the offices of Church and State.

St. Ambrose barring the emperor Theodosius from Milan Cathedral. After Constantine, the West would continue to contemplate the implication of Jesus' admonition to give to Caesar what belongs to Caesar and to God what belongs to God.

St. Benedict's monastery at Subiaco today. At Subiaco, and through his Rule, Benedict laid those solid foundations of Christian perfection on which he later would raise a spiritual building of lofty heights.

Oxford University, one of the first "lanterns in the house of God." The birth of the medieval universities was among the Church's most enduring gifts to the developing scientific culture of the West.

The Van Eyck brothers' 15th century *Ghent Altarpiece* offers a kind of summa on the Christian life.

The knight symbolizes the great movement within medieval Christendom to enact justice within the theatre of war. For all its flaws, the crusading enterprise helped inspire centuries of Christian thinking about the conduct in war whose mark is still felt in Western militaries; the fruits of these centuries of theory and practice, still ongoing, we call the "just war" tradition.

Against King Henry VIII (*above*), the Catholic Church remained as the one supranational authority that could check the ambitions that secular rulers held over their people; against John Calvin, cardinals and popes threw their enthusiasm behind the great renaissance artists such as Raphael, Bernini, and Caravaggio; against Luther (*below*), scholars like Erasmus upheld the freedom of the human will.

During the century and a half after the Protestant Reformation popes and bishops enlisted artists in the great effort at re-evangelizing Europe, launching the most exuberant expression the arts have ever known of which Caravaggio's *Crucifixion of St. Peter* (1601) is a fine example.

The interior of *Il Gesu*, the first Jesuit church in Rome, and the first, greatest expression of the new architecture of the Counter-reformation. In response to the Protestants, the Church answered with a three-pronged counter-thrust: the Council of Trent, the art of the Baroque, and the mission of the Jesuits.

After Cortez's conquests, the Spanish theologian Francesco di Vitoria and the Bishop Bartolomé Las Casas helped frame laws that protected the dignity and God-given rights of the people of New Spain. Contra Aristotle, the Church's best theologians argued there were no 'natural slaves.'

(*left*) Stained glass window of St. Kateri Tekakwitha; (*right*) painting of St. Isaac Jogues, S.J., one among the eight 17th century North American missionaries who served the Hurons and was martyred. Many among both the gift-givers and the gift-receivers paid dearly for the faith that was brought to the New World.

Liberty Guiding the People by Delacroix (1829). Concepts like universal rights, human dignity, social justice, and progress enter the vernacular of the West in the modern era. These are each terms that find their origins in Christian tradition. And yet they will be used, increasingly, for alien, and often destructive, purposes.

John Locke (1632-1704), one of the founders of modern secularism. For all John Locke's praise of religious toleration, he insisted that Catholics could never be loyal citizens of Britain.

It is as though Thérèse anticipated and experienced in herself all the tortured doubt, all the twisted anguish that the poison of public atheism would release into the atmosphere we moderns breathe.

Members of the Canadian Royal 22nd regiment, in audience with Pope Pius XII, following the 1944 liberation of Rome. During World War II the Allies and Pius XII collaborated in their campaign against the Nazis.

John Paul II's "Theology of the Body" has helped innumerable Christians embrace the Church's positive message of self-giving love.

But of course, Galileo was not alone in this conviction. Credible defenders of geocentricism, like the polymath French Jesuit Honoré Fabri (a theologian, mathematician, physicist, and zoologist who also independently discovered the circulation of the blood), had no quarrel with Galileo's principle. Indeed, *if* conclusive scientific evidence could be found in favor of a heliocentric cosmos, potentially conflicting passages would have to be interpreted, Fabri said, "figuratively."[12] The leading defender of orthodox theology of the time, St. Robert Bellarmine, had likewise urged caution. *If* strong scientific evidence seemed to conflict with an accepted (though not settled) interpretation of Scripture, then judgment should be withheld. Better "to say that we do not understand," Bellarmine argued, "rather than affirm as false what has been demonstrated."[13] And here is the point: Galileo's assertions were not yet demonstrated.

In the early years of his pontificate, John Paul II determined to revisit the judgment of Galileo's seventeenth-century ecclesiastical accusers. In 1981, he asked a special commission of scholars to re-examine the evidence surrounding Galileo's trial, an effort that concluded only after a decade of research. On October 31, 1992, the Holy Father convened a meeting with members of the Pontifical Academy of Sciences to receive the commission's findings. This was a long-anticipated moment. For centuries already, the Galileo affair had hung over the minds of many, clouding

---

282, cited in John Paul II, Allocution of October 31, 1992.

12 See Crombie, *Medieval and Early Modern Science,* vol. 2, 219.

13 Letter to Fr. A. Foscarini, 12 April 1615, cf. *Edizione nazionale delle Opere di Galileo Galilei* dir. A. Favaro vol. XII, p. 172, cited in John Paul II, Allocution of October 31, 1992.

their view of the Church's credibility. Before the pope, the commission delivered its conclusions. Despite the many complicating factors of the case, the Church, through her tribunal, had erred. In reply, the Holy Father thanked the commission for their effort, which, he suggested, "will be impossible to ignore in the future."

The condemnation was unfortunate. But the fruits of the lesson should not be lost. What was necessary was that both theologians and scientists maintain a scrupulous respect for the methods of the others' discipline. Man and the cosmos were too vast to be viewed from only one approach. Through the emergence of the scientific method in her midst, the Church had, over the past four hundred years, more clearly grasped distinctions between various disciplines. She had also learned to guard more carefully a rightful autonomy among sciences. "In fact," John Paul insisted, "the Bible does not concern itself with the details of the physical world, the understanding of which is the competence of human experience and reasoning." Even more, it was necessary for theologians to keep themselves "informed of scientific advances" in order to consider whether their own teachings needed reconsideration. In short, truth can never contradict truth.

While extending an apology, the pope also issued a challenge. Theology had grown in its self-understanding. The empirical sciences also needed to continue to grow in theirs. The universe is a cosmos, not a chaos. The very condition of scientific progress assumes truths elsewhere proved by philosophy; namely, the presence of the Creator. The enterprise of naming and then testing and confirming hypotheses presumes confidence in a rational order immanent within the universe. Ultimately, neither man nor the cosmos can be explained without acknowledging the Divine Reason standing behind regularities observed by reason. Scientists cannot afford to remain ignorant of their own presuppositions. This means that the scientist, as much as the theologian, must respect both the horizontal and the vertical modes of true progress. A civilization that excels at managing economies and diseases though ignorant of spiritual truth is a civilization sliding toward death. Thus John Paul called for the birth of a new humanism. He encouraged scientists to rediscover their appreciation for the grandeur of their work and for its just limits. Before the assembled audience of cardinals and scientists, he concluded: “Einstein used to say: ‘What is eternally incomprehensible in the world is that it is comprehensible.’ This intelligibility, attested to by the marvelous discoveries of science and technology, leads us, in the last analysis, to that transcendent and primordial Thought imprinted on all things.”[14]

~~~

But let us not get entangled. We may concede that, at least in part, the Galileo case is an unfortunate instance of the Church’s intervention at the dawn of early modern science. A larger question looms. Why did her culture produce scientists at all? Why Europe? Why should France or England or Italy develop the first universities and not one of the great cities of China or India or Egypt? Eastern

---

14 John Paul II, Allocution of October 31, 1992; see also George Weigel, *Witness to Hope*, 629–31.
~~~

civilizations had unified societies hundreds or even thousands of years older than Europe. Why were no universities born under Islam? John Paul II's philosophical reflections above point to an answer already evident to the historian. Two characteristics separated the culture of thirteenth-century Europe from both its neighbors and its predecessors: the extra-national character of the papacy and the Church's devotion to the unity of truth, natural and revealed.

If the papacy provided the condition for the institutional freedom of universities, the Church's devotion to truth provided its aboriginal motive. Freedom can always be negatively or positively defined. In the modern era, universities and their scholars typically understand their freedom in negative terms: freedom is freedom from authorities, freedom from constraints, freedom from belief in anything. That isn't the original sense of the term. Before anything else, intellectual freedom is a freedom to seek after and communicate truths found. It assumes, in other words, a prior confidence in the mind's capacity to know things—not that you or I (or anyone else) can gain a total grasp, but that man's intellectual appetite can, with reason, hope to find satisfaction in the good order of the cosmos. Only philosophy and theology can offer such ultimate assurances.

Far from hindering academic freedom, the Church's encouragement of theology provided for its possibility. To the medieval mind, theology was the freest of all the sciences. Many today would regard this claim as outrageous. But that is because most of us confuse the science of theology with mere "religiosity." For medieval intellectuals, theology was as much a science as is physics or chemistry or mathematics. Like these natural disciplines, theology, too, had its axioms, first principles, and rigorous methods. In fact, much of what passes as "scientific" discovery today—particularly in the realm of the social sciences—would have been ridiculed for its lack of rigor in the taverns and alleyways of fourteenth-century Oxford.

Besides being as scientifically rigorous as other disciplines, theology in the medieval view bears certain decisive advantages over the "hard" sciences. For starters, its object is more exalted. In this sense, theology is "freer" because its object can never be manipulated. Rocks, you can study to learn where to find fuel; plants, you might examine for medicine; men, you might even observe so as to learn how to govern; but God? No such motive can rationally apply. We can't control him. God we can only adore. Of course, Christians could look to the Bible for such an insight. But after the re-entry of Aristotle's writings on logic and physics into the West, Christian scholars could also look to an ancient source. As Aristotle or "the Philosopher"—as medieval scholars referred to him—insisted: of all the things men can know, theology is the best of all. "Evidently then we do not seek it for the sake of any other advantage; but as the man is free, we say, who exists for himself and not for another, so we pursue this as the only free science, for it alone exists for itself. . . . All the other sciences, indeed, are more necessary [to material life] than this, but none is better."[15]

Such was the fruit of enlightened pagan thinking. Christian philosophers went further. At Oxford, Paris, and across the continent, theology was called the queen of the sciences, not because she dominated other disciplines, but because

---

15 Aristotle, *Metaphysics*, trans. W. D. Ross, 1.2.

she served as the Lady of the great Manor of Learning. She was most beautiful to regard. She attracted and thus she organized. Her rule was not the sort of rule a general might exercise over his troops but more the way a tonic "rules" the chord or the way a center "rules" a circle's circumference.

To these medieval Christians, the liberal arts curriculum was often thought of as a circle, or a whole. The lower schools of the medieval university taught the seven liberal arts (grammar, rhetoric, logic, arithmetic, geometry, music, and astronomy), while the higher schools taught medicine, law, and theology. The division between the trivium and the quadrivium is principled. Where the first three disciplines give access to things insofar as they manifest differing qualities, the last four help us describe quantities. The liberal arts liberate through words and numbers. They liberate the mind so as to lead the student back to the first principle and end of things. As Hugh of St. Victor, an early professor from Paris, said in about 1130, by these seven arts, "a quick mind enters into the secret places of wisdom."[16] It was only after a long apprenticeship in the liberal arts that the student could turn to the more subtle questions of philosophy, and then, perhaps, of theology.

~~~

To illustrate the point, let us consider what actually took place in a medieval classroom. When Thomas Aquinas left the monastic school established at Monte Cassino, motherhouse of the Benedictines, he was about fourteen.

---

16 Hugh of St. Victor, *Didascalicon: On the Study of Reading*, trans. Taylor, 3.3.
~~~

From there, he entered the newly established University of Naples in 1239. Here Thomas continued his studies in logic, grammar, natural philosophy, and ethics. Early university documents give us a reasonable picture of the sorts of basic philosophical texts that Thomas and students after him would have heard lectures on, including the following:

- Porphyry, *Isagoge* (logic);
- Boethius, *Topics* (logic);
- Aristotle, *Physics*, *Generation and Corruption*, books 1–2 (physics);
- Averroes, *On the substance of the world* (physics);
- Aristotle, *Meteorology*, *On the Soul* (psychology), *Metaphysics*, books 1, 2, 5–12 (philosophy);
- Aristotle, *Posterior and Prior Analytics* (logic), *Rhetoric*, *Politics* (politics and ethics), and *Economic*s.

Such texts formed a sort of common core, properly understood. Through these masterpieces, students were introduced to the rigorous demands of logic and definition, the first principles of physics, astronomy, ethics, politics, and psychology. Of course, students focusing on medicine or astrology or law or theology would encounter many other books, such as those by Galen, Hippocrates, Euclid, Ptolemy, Gratian, or the *Sentences* of Peter Lombard.[17]

At Naples, Thomas got to know not only Aristotle but a new order of religious named after their founder, Dominic Guzman. The Dominicans had been approved by the pope only a few years earlier in 1216, the same year that the

---

17 This list I derive from two documentary statutes, one from the University of Paris (1255), another from the University of Bologna (1405), which form the earliest complete statutes, Malagola, ed., *Statuti dell'universitat e dei collegii dello studio Bolognese*, 1888, in Thorndike, *University Records*, 64-66 and 273-82.

followers of Francis of Assisi received recognition. Like the Franciscans, the Dominicans were a mendicant order. Unlike Benedictines, who lived off of the revenues of cultivated properties, these new kind of religious traveled from town to town begging for their bread in exchange for their preaching (*mendicans* in Latin means "begging").

Thomas came from a powerful aristocratic family. His mother nurtured higher ambitions for her precocious boy and would have none of such foolishness. Upon hearing news of her son's departure with the Dominicans, she sent guards after him. She had the young man imprisoned in their family castle for two years. She even brought a woman into his room to see if natural enticements might clear his head of his evangelical fervor. It is said that Thomas chased the girl out with a stick. Except for his devout sister, no other visitors disturbed him, nor did Thomas remain idle. While patiently awaiting freedom, he spent these days praying, reading the Bible, and absorbing the leading work of theology of the time, Peter Lombard's *Sentences*. Eventually his mother did relent. When she did, Thomas was free to return to the Dominicans. In 1245, at the age of twenty, he found himself in the center of the intellectual revival in Christendom, Paris.[18]

Besides lecture and exegesis, the distinguishing method of the medieval schools, already well established at Paris, was the disputation. As the typical mode for treating advanced problems, Western universities kept up some form of the procedure for about five hundred years. On special

---

18 For background to Thomas's education and bibliographical information, see Vivian Boland, *St. Thomas Aquinas* (London: Continuum, 2007).

days through the calendar (especially during high liturgical seasons), masters and students would gather to hear participants debate a "disputed question." To begin, there was the question itself. It had to be manageable. Instead of asking whether it is permissible to pollute the environment, you might ask the more moderately sized question, such as, "Whether it is ever environmentally responsible to own, as a commuting vehicle, an F-150 Ford Truck?" A small number of senior students or faculty would treat opposite sides to the question. Terms like "environmentally responsible" and "ownership" would be clarified. Distinctions, as in this case, between the primary and secondary uses of a vehicle could be teased out, the benefits of domestic versus foreign ownership articulated, and conclusions drawn.

The next day the "magister," or senior lecturer, would then provide his so called "resolution" of the opposing arguments. His first step would be to summarize the best *opposing* arguments to his own conclusion ("since F-150s use gasoline instead of electricity, they ought to be banned"); next, he would cite an authority that favored his own position ("but many good men drive such trucks"); then, he would offer his rational case, moving from premises to conclusion, and round up the discussion by answering the objections he earlier raised. You get some idea of the riotous fun that must have been had when you look at a text like St. Thomas's *Disputed Questions on Truth*, a reproduction of the experience of the disputations that he participated in during the winter term of 1250 at the University of Paris.

Some sense of the medieval love of dialectical reasoning, of considering alternative propositions, can be seen from the writings of its great masters. Anselm's (1033–1109) *Prosologion* seeks, through the contemplation of the idea of God, to prove his existence. Abelard's (1079–1142) early work *Sic et Non* ("*Yes and No*") is an exercise in reconciling apparently contradictory claims. Greatest of all the scholastics, though, was St. Thomas, and greatest among all his works was the *Summa Theologica.*

The book is organized with all the symmetry of a Gothic cathedral. The very structure of the *Summa* expresses the medieval passion for organization and logical clarity. Its three parts deal with God, man, and man's return to happiness through Christ. Within these parts there are 38 logically contained treatises, 631 questions, roughly 10,000 objections, all of which are built off individual "articles"—3,000 of them. Each article again is subdivided into discrete units. First, statements of the best opposing views to Thomas's own. Then, a reference to some authority that seems to suggest otherwise than his opponents. Next, his own logical reply. Finally, a statement of resolution, where the merits and deficiencies of the opening objections are sorted. Here is Aquinas's first article of the majestic *Summa Theologica*, in which he asks: "Whether, besides philosophy, any further doctrine is required." The gist of the question is as follows. If philosophy already has methods for examining the first principles of all things, including up to God himself, why do we need revelation?

> ***Objection 1:*** It seems that, besides philosophical science, we have no need of any further knowledge. For man should not seek to know what is above reason: "Seek not the things that are too high for thee" (Ecclus. 3:22). But whatever is not above reason is fully treated of in philosophical science.

Therefore any other knowledge besides philosophical science is superfluous.

Objection 2: Further, knowledge can be concerned only with being, for nothing can be known, save what is true; and all that is, is true. But everything that is, is treated of in philosophical science—even God Himself; so that there is a part of philosophy called theology, or the divine science, as Aristotle has proved (Metaph. vi). Therefore, besides philosophical science, there is no need of any further knowledge.

On the contrary, It is written (2 Tim 3:16): "All Scripture, inspired of God is profitable to teach, to reprove, to correct, to instruct in justice." Now Scripture, inspired of God, is no part of philosophical science, which has been built up by human reason. Therefore it is useful that besides philosophical science, there should be other knowledge, i.e. inspired of God.

I answer that, It was necessary for man's salvation that there should be a knowledge revealed by God besides philosophical science built up by human reason. Firstly, indeed, because man is directed to God, as to an end that surpasses the grasp of his reason: "The eye hath not seen, O God, besides Thee, what things Thou hast prepared for them that wait for Thee" (Is 66:4). But the end must first be known by men who are to direct their thoughts and actions to the end. Hence it was necessary for the salvation of man that certain truths which exceed human reason should be made known to him by divine revelation. Even as regards those truths about God which human reason could have discovered, it was necessary that man should be taught by a divine revelation; because the truth about God such as reason could discover, would only be known by a few, and that after a long time, and with the admixture of many errors. Whereas man's whole salvation, which is in God, depends upon the knowledge of this truth. Therefore, in order that the salvation of men might be brought about more fitly and more surely, it was necessary that they should be taught divine truths by divine revelation. It was therefore necessary that besides philosophical science built up by reason, there should be a sacred science learned through revelation.

Reply to Objection 1: Although those things which are beyond man's knowledge may not be sought for by man through his reason, nevertheless, once they are revealed by God, they must be accepted by faith. Hence the sacred text continues, "For many things are shown to thee above the understanding of man" (Ecclus. 3:25). And in this, the sacred science consists.

Reply to Objection 2: Sciences are differentiated according to the various means through which knowledge is obtained. For the astronomer and the physicist both may prove the same conclusion: that the earth, for instance, is round: the astronomer by means of mathematics (i.e. abstracting from matter), but the physicist by means of matter itself. Hence there is no reason why those things which may be learned from philosophical science, so far as they can be known by natural reason, may not also be taught us by another science so far as they fall within revelation. Hence theology included in sacred doctrine differs in kind from that theology which is part of philosophy.

~~~

Unlike at today's universities, virtually no questions were barred. The whole procedure was meant to put reason to the test from every imaginable point of view. If it does not surprise that the first to mount a legal defense of academic freedom was a pope, it is no wonder that it was another bishop of Rome, John XXI, who would write the first definitive textbook for formal logic in the 1230s. So popular was his work, *Summulae logicales*, that by the seventeenth century it had gone through some 166 editions.[19]

By contrast, universities of the modern era are not so bold. The shift in their guiding purpose can be understood,

---

19 On this, see Edward Grant, *God and Reason in the Middle Ages* (Cambridge: Cambridge University Press, 2001), 116.
~~~

in part, by the shift in their patronage. It was on the European continent, during the period of the French Revolution, that the institutions first saw their decline. Not only were all Church properties confiscated by Napoleon; he also shut the doors of theological institutions, including, at the heart of the University of Paris, the prestigious college of the Sorbonne. Protestant Germany followed suit. Prior to 1789, some thirty-two medieval universities existed in Germany. During the next generation, about half were dissolved, among these, nine sponsored by the Catholic Church.[20] By the late nineteenth and early twentieth centuries, instead of teaching and the arts, instead of the generous study of ultimate questions, purely mechanical disciplines began to assume a central role. The university became an arm of the state. Money and prestige now flow to special research centers where industrial farming techniques, weapons, and useful medicines are developed.

Who isn't pleased with penicillin? No doubt we benefit enormously from the fruits of applied science. But our medicines and bombs and chips have been bought at a cost. Specialization has grown up alongside fragmentation. What students can no longer expect from the university is to encounter a *uni*verse. As Binx Bolling, the wandering exile of Walker Percy's *The Moviegoer*, puts it after completing a ravenous course of study: "The only difficulty was that though the universe had been disposed of, I myself was left over."[21] That names the problem. Without theology, without a queen, the many lesser disciplines and the study of

---

20 See Thomas Albert Howard, *Protestantism and the Rise of the Modern German University* (Oxford: Oxford University Press, 2006), 134–37.

21 Walker Percy, *The Moviegoer* (New York: Knopf, 1961), 70.

their practical applications seem to have gone each their own way, like children without a mother, without hope of ever finding home. It's common for biologists today to know nothing about history, and to find English majors who barely know how to add, for psychologists to deny the soul, and philosophy majors to doubt whether there's anything outside of their own head. Sense and sensibility have been sundered. Having abandoned theology, having abandoned a science of first principles, the university today is better thought of as a *multiversity*: a place where you can ask nearly any question you want, well, except of course, whether feminism is true, and whether life is worth living.

Parents and grandparents think they know what goes on inside college classrooms because they (or one of their siblings) went to college in the sixties or seventies or eighties. But, in fact, they usually don't know. The brick and stone of their alma mater might look pretty much like they did forty years ago; but what goes on inside may surprise. No, their Johnny or Susan or Tiffany likely won't have to learn a foreign language, or logic, or Shakespeare, but they will learn a lot of cool stuff our grandparents never heard of. For example, here's a description of a few of the trendy courses you can take at elite universities these days.[22] From Brown University's official description of the course: "Global Macho: Race, Gender, and Action Movies" (3 credits, $7,925). "Carefully sifting through an oft-overlooked but globally popular genre—the muscle-bound action [film]—this class asks: what sort of work does an action movie do?

[22] These figures and descriptions are helpfully compiled by John Zmirak in "Seven Ridiculous Courses at Top Colleges" in *Intercollegiate Review* (Spring 2015).

What is the role of women in this genre? . . . How should we think critically about movies that feature—often without apology—a deep, dangerous obsession with masculinity, patriarchy, war, and lawlessness, with violence outside of civil society?"

At Brown you can learn why guys like watching things blow up. Well, at Bryn Mawr College, no one has to read John Milton, but you can fulfill the college's single required literature course by trying out this one: "Queens, Nuns, and Other Deviants in the Early Modern Iberian World" (3 credits, $7,353). Last, but hardly least expensive, there's Georgetown, America's flagship university in the so-called Jesuit-light tradition. Everyone at Georgetown needs to take a little theology. Most of us like dogs. Here's where a Catholic university can fill a gap. One of the options your son or daughter can select for satisfying their theology requirement is "Dogs and Theology" (3 credits, $7,453). Who hasn't wondered where his grandfather's German Shepherd ended up?

But we must move along. Far from hindering science, the Catholic Church, virtually alone among institutions, provided the necessary conditions that made possible its rebirth in the Middle Ages and Renaissance. On the one hand, Catholic theology declares the unity of all knowledge, natural and revealed. This faith supplied the hope that scientists needed and still need in their quest for a coherent account of nature. On the other hand, Catholic polity establishes the liberty of the pope against secular rulers, now and till the return of Christ. This confidence supplied the stability that scholars needed and still need in their quest for academic communities not tied to the vicissitudes of politics.

Post-Christian nihilism is arguably our culture's greatest enemy of intellectual freedom today; but in the Middle Ages, while the university ministered to the mind, the body of Christendom was being attacked by a new and powerful society whose creed was simple and whose armies were fierce.

6

CRUSADERS: THE GIFTS OF CHRISTIAN WARRIORS

"Knighthood has blossomed forth into new life."

St. Bernard of Clairvaux

POPES these days don't call for crusades. There are sensible reasons for this. Nevertheless, the resurgence of a militant Islam has forced both the devout and the indifferent in the West to reconsider the legacy of the crusaders and the ideals for which their armies fought. Despite the many tragedies and failures of the Holy Wars that Christians would fight against Islam—and there were many of each—the first gift the Church's knights, her crusaders, offered to the West was this: political freedom. The crusaders saved Europe from being absorbed into a caliphate, a Muslim dominated territory, of the sort that is being imposed upon Middle Eastern Christians today. When viewed in their historical context, the Crusades were as much wars of liberation as they were acts of self-defense against a hostile civilization; had the soldiers of Gaul, Normandy, Flanders, the Rhine, and England not armed and faced east, the mighty stream that became the West would have been divided into a dozen wandering rivulets and perhaps evaporated forever. And so it may truly be said that we owe many of the inherited political freedoms we cherish to the sacrifices and heroism of the men who took up the cross in defense of Christendom.

But our political freedom under God is not the only gift bequeathed to us as a result of the Crusades. To point to the other chief gift, I enlist the aid of a visual masterpiece of the early fifteenth century, the Van Eyck brothers' *Ghent Altarpiece*. This multi-paneled work offers a kind of summa on the Christian life. At its center sits the famous image of the adoration of the lamb, surrounded by angels holding instruments of the Passion. Adam and Eve flank the top panels, followed by angels in choir, the Baptist, the Virgin Mary, and God the Father. The lower panels depict the various ranks of Christians parading in procession toward the lamb, themselves representing the cardinal virtues. Hermits for temperance, pilgrims for prudence, judges for justice, and beside them, embodying courage, the *milites Christi*, the soldiers of Christ. The Church's direction in the European crusading effort helped discipline the warrior and convert him into a justly romanticized figure, the knight. The knight symbolizes the great movement within medieval Christendom to enact justice within the theatre of war. If men were to fight in defense of Christian causes, they would have to submit themselves to the rigors of the Gospel. Of course, individual knights could falter. But the crusading enterprise helped inspire an ethic and give impetus to centuries of Christian thinking about conduct in war, the mark of which is still felt in Western militaries; the fruits of these centuries of theory and practice, still ongoing, we call the just war tradition. In our reflections on the crusading movement, we'll consider both of the aforementioned gifts.

~~~

But perhaps another preamble is needed before we turn to the details. Even more than the condemnation of Galileo, there are few episodes that Marxist and Whig progressive historians love to hate as much as this. Popular imagination has been so saturated with the myth of the injustice of the Crusades that a fair examination of the details of this several-hundred-year event is difficult. Intensity of feeling often gets in the way of historical honesty. I cite two instances. At the turn of the new millennium, and only months before Muslim terrorists would drive commercial airliners into the World Trade Center's twin towers, several hundred Protestants joined in a "reconciliation walk" that took them from Germany to the Holy Land. They wore messages that said "I apologize" in Arabic. The march marked the nine hundredth anniversary of the crusaders' conquest of Jerusalem. It was intended as an act of reparation for crimes of medieval soldiers. An official statement explained their motivations: "Nine hundred years ago, our forefathers carried the name of Jesus Christ in battle across the Middle East. Fueled by fear, greed, and hatred. . . . We deeply regret the atrocities committed in the name of Christ by our predecessors. We renounce greed, hatred and fear, and condemn all violence done in the name of Jesus Christ."[1]

And then another example. Weeks after the attack, a similar message about the Crusades was conveyed from another quarter. In a lecture delivered November 7, 2001, at Georgetown University, former American president Bill Clinton tried to account for the terrorist attack on the

---

1 For the manifesto, see religioustolerance.org/chr_cru1.htm.
~~~

United States, in part, by saying that it was an answer by Muslims against Christians. The terror that the crusaders inflicted nearly a millennium ago incurred a debt, he said, "and we are still paying for it."[2] Were the Crusades an act of self-serving violence upon a peaceful and enlightened culture? Were they, as the popular religious writer and ex-nun Karen Armstrong has insisted, Christian Europe's first attack against relatively harmonious foreigners?[3] Were they the West's first act of "colonization"?

Outside of trendy "peace-studies" programs, it's less common these days to hear the refrain that Islam is a religion of peace. According to one international watch-group, between September 11, 2001 and the end of 2017, Islamic terrorists have committed some 32,315 deadly strikes, or about five per day.[4] Many Muslims do wish to live

---

2 A cheap shot made in a speech not without some merits. For the transcript, see http://ecumene.org/clinton.htm.

3 See Karen Armstrong, *Holy War: The Crusades and Their Impact on Today's World* (New York: Random House, 2001). In the first thousand years, in her telling, European Christians did a pretty good job at keeping Christianity "a religion of love and peace." After Pope Urban's call to arms, they gave in. Following in the steps of a "Jungian archetype," Western Christians tried but failed to hold out against their own native "compulsion" toward violence (p. 4). And thus, in one former nun's telling, began the Crusades.

4 These statistics compiled by *The Religion of Peace*, a non-partisan organization tracking the effects of global jihadism. See their website https://www.thereligionofpeace.com/pages/site/the-list.aspx for their definitions and sources. I note that in 2004 the BBC, in partnership with a research group from King's College London, conducted its independent analysis of Jihadist attacks. For the month of November of that year, the BBC found 664 attacks resulting in 5042 deaths—the majority of which were civilian, delivered by bullets or bombs, including 38 suicide attacks (see http://www.bbc.com/news/world-30080914). By

peaceably. Some make the case for a spiritual interpretation of jihad. Others look to Turkey as a model of a culturally Muslim, politically secular state (although that model seems increasingly less secure). Peering across the next fifty years, we in the West must pray that such voices win the debate over how Muslims can forge a peaceful coexistence with their neighbors. At a recent address to religious scholars at Al-Azhar University, the foremost academy in the Arabic world, the president of Egypt, Al-Sisi, warned that extremism within Islam is a threat to peace everywhere. The president exhorted his fellow Muslims:

> It is inconceivable that the ideology we sanctify should make our entire nation a source of concern, danger, killing, and destruction all over the world. . . . It has reached the point that [this ideology] is hostile to the entire world. Is it conceivable that 1.6 billion [Muslims] would kill the world's population of 7 billion, so that they could live [on their own]? This is inconceivable. I say these things here, at Al-Azhar, before religious clerics and scholars. May Allah bear witness on Judgment Day to the truth of your intentions, regarding what I say to you today. You cannot see things clearly when you are locked [in this ideology]. You must emerge from it and look from outside, in order to get closer to a truly enlightened ideology. You must oppose it with resolve. Let me say it again: We need to revolutionize our religion. Honorable Imam [the Grand Sheik of Al-Azhar], you bear responsibility before Allah. The world in its entirety awaits your words, because the Islamic nation is being torn apart, destroyed, and is heading to perdition. We ourselves are bringing it to perdition.[5]

---

way of contrast, the tally made by *The Religion of Peace* for that same period counted fewer than half the attacks and deaths (284 and 2,515 respectively) than the tally arrived at by the BBC.

5 Citation reported in Robert R. Reilly, "Isis the Irrational," in *Intercollegiate Review* (Fall 2015).

We must work and pray to support such voices within the Islamic world today. As a matter of historical fact, however, Islam has rarely found a way to disentangle its religion from its politics. One reason for this is that, for several hundred years, within Sunni Islam, at least, the dominant view is that nothing mediates between the commands of God and the laws of men. In the West, the natural law tradition developed as a way to reconcile faith, reason, and politics; no parallel development has occurred in Islam.

Had Europe not repelled the Muslims, it is not difficult to imagine the future that could have been. Counterfactual reasoning in this case is possible because of a peculiar feature of Islamic societies: compared to European countries, they look today roughly how they looked six hundred years ago. Nearly all the fruits of civilization that we in the West cherish, from representative government and advanced technology, to freedom of speech, to the music of Mozart, to baseball and ice-hockey, to economic and religious liberty, would never have developed had the West succumbed. Thanks in large measure to the popes, we never did.

~~~

On November 27, 1095, Pope Urban II stepped onto a large platform amidst a sea of men who had gathered outside of the French city of Claremont. A council had just been convened. The pope had renewed his censure against King Philip of France for violating his marriage covenant, but another, larger, crisis loomed. Urban II also called the nobles and feudal lords together in response to a letter. Urban received a message from the Byzantine emperor
~~~

Alexius Comnenus. It was an impassioned plea for charity. Muslim armies were poised once more to attack. Christian brothers, the emperor warned, were in danger of being slaughtered. The only man capable of uniting the scattered nobility of Europe and gathering support for a military mission that would call men thousands of miles away from their homes was, of course, the pope. Christendom's spiritual leader accepted the embattled emperor's call for help. On that November afternoon, Pope Urban II made good on his intention to intervene. He called representatives of Christian Europe to assemble. On that platform he launched the First Crusade.

In vivid detail, the Holy Father conjured before this immense crowd images of torture, rape, and the desecration of churches. "They have killed and captured many, and have destroyed the churches and devastated the empire." Greek Christians were under siege, but the whole of Christendom would suffer outrage: "If you permit them to continue thus for awhile with impunity, the faithful of God will be much more widely attacked by them." And then, before that crowd of gathered nobles and peasants, the Vicar of Christ called upon Christians to wage a holy war of liberation with these words:

> They have occupied more and more of the lands of those Christians, and have overcome them in seven battles. They have killed and captured many, and have destroyed the churches and devastated the empire. If you permit them to continue thus for awhile with impunity, the faithful of God will be much more widely attacked by them. On this account I, or rather the Lord, beseech you as Christ's heralds to publish this everywhere and to persuade all people of whatever rank, foot-soldiers and knights, poor and rich, to carry aid promptly

> to those Christians and to destroy that vile race from the lands of our friends. I say this to those who are present, it is meant also for those who are absent. Moreover, Christ commands it.[6]

With rapturous cries, the crowd yelled out *Deus vult, Deus vult,* "God wills it! God wills it!" Thus began the European Crusades.

Let's begin with a definition. As an historical phenomenon, the Crusades describe a series of military campaigns between Christian and Islamic armies over control of the Holy Land between 1095 and 1291. I do not propose to narrate the details of these conflicts, nor a defense of the crusaders' conduct in each of the wars; I wish merely to show that for their chief successes we should feel gratitude, and for many of their ideals, admiration.

In general, historians divide the drama of the Crusades into eight acts. Some of these, like the First Crusade (1096–99), were outstanding military successes. In this initial campaign, Christian armies assembled at Constantinople in 1096. The following spring, they freed the ancient Christian city of Nicaea (where Constantine held the first ecumenical Church council); then they freed Antioch in 1098 (that's the city where believers were first called Christians, cf. Acts 11:26) and subsequently Jerusalem in 1099 (where Jesus was crucified). After these victories, some of the

---

[6] Taken from Bongars, *Gesta Dei per Francos*, trans. in Oliver J. Thatcher and Edgar Holmes McNeal, eds., *A Source Book for Medieval History* (New York: Scribners, 1905), 513–17. Five versions of Pope Urban's call to the Crusades were recorded and can be found, as was the above, at Fordham University's online Medieval Sourcebook http://sourcebooks.fordham.edu/halsall/source/urban2-5vers.asp#gesta.

nobles stayed behind. Understandably, they established a number of crusader states. These were necessary to maintain control over the recovered territories. In essence, all further Crusades were launched to deflect attacks against these newly recovered sites.

Other campaigns, like the Fourth Crusade (1202–4), were disasters. It was during this venture into Christendom's eastern capital that a disorganized and underfunded band of recruits was deceived and then seduced—partly through the greed of Venetian officials, partly through the cunning of the exiled emperor of Constantinople, and partly through their own stupidity—into doing some freelance work along the way to Jerusalem against the pope's explicit orders. Hence, in place of legitimate enemies, this renegade force, in 1204, sacked Constantinople instead and then set up Western rule in the city for the next half century, an affront that Eastern Christians would not soon forget.

~~~

Was war between Islam and the West inevitable? Not really. Prior to Muhammad's birth, Christian peoples inhabited the extensive lands of the Roman Empire. Christian territory included the eastern cities of Bagdad, Alexandria, and Jerusalem. In the eighty years after Mohammed's death in 632, not only were these ancient Christian cities overrun, but so also was all of Christian North Africa and most of Spain. In the course of a century, the eastern Roman Empire, and with it a civilization nourished by centuries of Christian martyrs, missionaries, and mystics, had been razed or enslaved by Muslim armies.
~~~

At no point during the early conquests did the West significantly interfere. In part, this was because the West was divided. After the fall of Rome in 410, political unity was slow to return to the West. Italy, along with the provinces of Germany, France, and Spain, had been divided up by various barbarian successor kingdoms whose attachment to orthodox Christianity varied more or less according to the centuries. Yet the fact stands. For roughly four hundred years, Christians in the West tolerated Muslim control of vast sections of the Middle East. I emphasize this to illustrate an historical truth. Western Christian "fear, greed, and hatred" seems hardly adequate to account for the launch of such a campaign hundreds of years after the initial attack. As it happens, credible proximate causes can be found.

What more directly precipitated the crisis was a change in Muslim policy. Since the time of Constantine—who, along with his mother, Helena, lavishly funded churches in Jerusalem—Christians had been making pilgrimages to Palestine as acts of prayer and penance. Much like a parish priest might today, St. Jerome, to offer one fourth-century example, led a small group of pilgrims on a tour from Rome to the Holy Land. After guiding the tour, Jerome stayed on. So did others. His patroness, a wealthy widow named Paula, financed the construction of a monastery for Jerome and a few others near Bethlehem. It was during these last thirty-two years of retirement that Jerome would translate the Bible from Greek and Hebrew into Latin.

From the early centuries of the Church, then, Palestine had always supported a strong Christian presence. Muslim conquests of the Holy Land in the seventh century did little to change this. The process of Islamicization of conquered lands was slow and uneven. For those Christians and Jews living within Islamic-controlled territory, the so-called *Dar al-Islam* (House of Islam), religious toleration was declared within certain early Islam texts. In exchange for toleration, the People of the Book had to accept their position as subordinates and pay a tax, the *jizya*.[7] Thus, even after the Arabic conquest, Christian pilgrims and their money were accepted in the Holy City. Except for occasional outbursts of killings and the destruction of churches, Christians were for the most part left in peace.[8] After 1076, the situation for Christians grew intolerable. A new Muslim ruler had conquered the city. Now began in earnest an unprecedented round of Muslim attacks. Christian sites were destroyed. Pilgrims were rebuffed. Travelers brought home tales of bloodshed. It is this turn in policy, as well as the plea for help from Constantinople, that precipitated the start of Western military involvement.[9]

Catholics often wince at the mention of these medieval battles. That is, on the whole, a symptom of false guilt. Since the eighteenth century, Western condemnations of the Crusades have been common. This is not true among Muslims; evidently, the majority of Muslims, up until about one hundred years ago, remembered them largely as victories. Unqualified indignation issued first from the

---

7 For background, see Christopher Tyerman's magisterial *God's War: A New History of the Crusades* (Cambridge, MA: Harvard University Press, 2006), 51–53.

8 Examples and references are multiplied, for instance, in Rodney Stark, *God's Battalions: The Case for the Crusades* (New York: Harper One, 2009), 85.

9 For background, see Daniel-Rops, *Cathedral and Crusade*, 433–35.

proselytizers for the Enlightenment and architects of the anti-clerical French Revolution. Hence, Voltaire (1694–1778) called them "an epidemic of fury which lasted for two hundred years"; for David Hume (1711–76) they were "the most durable monument to human folly"; for Denis Diderot (1713–84) they dragged "a significant part of the world into an unhappy little country in order to cut the inhabitants' throats."[10] Later historians would pick up on the theme of the crusaders' colonial ambitions, and of their quest for prosperity. None of these images render justice. Over the last sixty years, such simplistic pictures have been overturned. Among scholars, at least, the thesis of brutish Normans disrupting an enlightened eastern civilization has been undermined. The forces and ideas that produced the crusading effort are, in fact, amazingly varied—as should be expected from a movement that spanned several hundred years. To take just one example, it is hardly believable that money was a prime motivator. We have records of entire families selling their properties at below costs so as to amass enough capital for the arduous pilgrimage. An early crusading song put it, "There we must go, selling our goods to buy the temple of God and to destroy the Saracens."[11] Political and economic causes, to some degree and in certain cases, motivated, but righteous, religious, and romantic reasons mattered more. In the eyes of the key Western actors—chiefly, the popes—the crusades were launched on behalf of beleaguered brethren in battles of

---

10 These taken from Stark, *God's Battalions*, 6.

11 For an excellent discussion of the primary sources, see Christopher Tyerman, *God's War*, 83–89.

self-defense against an expansionist empire whose hunger for conquest had not yet abated.

Materialist historical assumptions can only lead one so far. To interpret the interactions between medieval Muslims and Christians, eventually one must take into account religion. And so, while it is true that the Crusades can be usefully contained within a two-hundred-year period, the larger conflict between Christianity and Islam cannot. Christians won empire through martyrdom. Muslims gained theirs through more conventional means, shaving off the limbs of a civilization that had shared a common faith for four centuries and a common border since Caesar Augustus. In contemporary accounts of the Crusades, one rarely hears of the "scandal" of Islam's rapid and brutal colonial expansionism. At the time of the first Muslim invasions into the Roman Empire, Christianity had been the "native" religion of the eastern Mediterranean cities for more than twice as long as the United States of America has been a nation.

Differences in the two religion's early expansions can partially be explained by differences in the characters of their respective founders. In Muslim tradition, Muhammad's life is customarily divided into two phases: the Medina period and the Mecca period. These refer to the first and second phases of his public work. The first period marks the years shortly after Muhammad experienced what he regarded as a sequence of revelations in about AD 610. The sonorous utterances he heard in his ear initially terrified him. He eventually accepted them in peace. Once he began preaching, he asked others to do the same. At first, it was impossible for Muhammad to gather an armed force. During these years, he also preached a more pacific message. It is from this period that you can find the texts in the Koran that sound like Surah 2:256, "There is no compulsion in religion." In his second period, his message changed. AD 622 marks the start of Muhammed's residence in Medina and the first year of the Islamic calendar. It is from this second period that we find texts in the Koran such as Surah 9:73 "O Prophet! Make war on the unbelievers and the hypocrites. Be harsh with them. Their ultimate abode is hell, a hapless journey's end." Those who argue that such texts, and the call to jihad throughout the Koran, are meant to be taken "spiritually" might have something interesting to offer Islam. But they do not represent its dominant historical self-understanding. Nor do they match up with the prophet's own action. During Muhammad's Medina period, he consolidated power and was not afraid to exile opponents, enslave them, or have them executed.[12]

Thus, where the Jewish Messiah carried a cross for his love for mankind, the Muslim prophet preached jihad; where Jesus submitted to a horrific death on a cross, Muhammed commanded armies; and where Catholic political theory divides authority between sacred and secular rulers, Muslims have sought a unified caliphate. Beyond being fundamentally defensive battles, battles waged to keep a hostile civilization at bay, and to keep available access to historically Christian sites, the Church found a way to bring a measure of nobility even to bloody warfare.

---

12 For orientation, see *The Oxford History of Islam*, ed. John L. Esposito (Oxford: Oxford University Press, 1999), 10.

Christ never asked soldiers to renounce their profession. What he did tell them was that they must love their enemies. Believers must obey earthly rulers, St. Peter insisted, but they are to do so as "aliens and exiles" who belong to another country (1 Pt 2:11). The Catholic approach to war and peace is not a matter of embracing either/or but rather of accepting both/and. If you are a Christian, you are obliged *both* to pay Caesar's tax *and* to bind yourself to a higher code. If you are a soldier, you may be called, like St. Sebastian, both to fight for the earthly city and to burn as an innocent martyr for the heavenly one. St. Louis of France died pursuing the first call; St. Francis of Assisi wanted nothing more than to answer the second.

~~~

If the first gift of the Crusades was political and economic, the second was moral and imaginative. Beyond defending the freedom of the West, the popes' encouragement of the Crusades taught active men how to channel their energy into noble forms of service.

War demands sacrifice. That demand could be elevated to the level of grace. The era from the eleventh through the thirteenth centuries marked the height of chivalry. The knight was taught that his first duty was to protect the weak and to apply his force within the bounds of justice. It is from this era that the popular legends of the Knights of the Round Table emerge. Thomas Aquinas, drawing on Augustine, expressed conditions that had to be met for war to be justified: only the public authority can declare war, it must be engaged for just reasons, waging war must
~~~

promise reasonable prospect of success, and so on.[13] But Thomas, in one way, is merely the beginning of a more complete development of the just war tradition. The whole pursuit of war, in the developing Christian imagination, came to be understood in judicial terms. Concepts like the discriminate and proportionate use of force became finely tuned instruments in other hands. The Spanish theologian Francesco di Vitoria (1485–1546), one of the fathers of international law, articulated this position when he argued: "The victor must think of himself as a judge sitting in judgment between two commonwealths, one the injured party and the other the offender; he must not pass sentence as the prosecutor, but as a judge. He must give satisfaction to the injured, but as far as possible without causing the utter ruination of the guilty commonwealth."[14]

Not even the experience of war can suspend the obligations of the Gospel. War must only be pursued in the cause of justice. Some Christians today would undoubtedly prefer to return to the pacific stand of the early Church, when Christian involvement in the pagan army was generally discouraged; but that would be tantamount to saying that Christ has no wisdom to offer Caesar. It would, in short, be simply to allow war-making to return to where Enlightenment secular theorists and rulers dragged her in the nineteenth and twentieth centuries, and to the Machiavellian wisdom of Carl von Clausewitz who, in his influential

---

13 See his *Summa Theologica* II-II q.40 a.1.

14 Di Vitoria, *De iure belli relectio* 3.9.60 in *Vitoria: Political Writings*, ed. A. Pagden and J. Lawrance (Cambridge: Cambridge University Press, 1991); I have benefited here from Oliver O'Donovan, *The Just War Revisited* (Cambridge: Cambridge University Press, 2003).

textbook on military strategy, *On War*, declared: "War is only a continuation of state policy by other means."[15]

On the ethics of war, the Church in the twenty-first century continues to offer advice to Caesar. Western militaries to this day issue to their troops ROEs (Rules of Engagement) that legally define, and often radically curtail, the sorts of violence that may be used against enemies. Western multinational covenants, like the Hague Conventions (1899, 1907) and now the Geneva Convention (1949), bind Western soldiers and commanders to disciplines—such as the avoidance of targeting civilians—that were unheard of in ancient Greece and find little support among non-Western nations. The roots of these sentiments go back to this late medieval and early modern tradition.

But to return to the era of the Crusades, yet another fruit of the Church's effort to subject war to the Gospel's discipline was the birth of a group of soldiers whose deeds would become the subject of thrilling legends and novels: the Knights of the Temple. The Knights of the Temple would become rich and powerful but began poor and insignificant, at least in the eyes of the world. Nine French knights founded the brotherhood at Jerusalem in 1118 for the protection of Christian pilgrims. The great mystic St. Bernard was present when the pope gave these knights official standing in the Church. He even penned their code, modeling it after his own Cistercian Rule. In his *In Praise of the New Knighthood*, St. Bernard expressed the lofty ideal to which these Christian warriors were to aspire. "In

---

15 See Carl von Clausewitz's *On War*, ed. and trans. Howard and Paret (New Jersey: University of Princeton Press, 1989), 40.

this Order," he wrote, "knighthood has blossomed forth into new life: warriors whose sole aim in life it once was to rob, to plunder, and to kill, have now bound themselves by solemn vow to defend the poor and the Church."[16]

Two other orders born during the Crusades expressed this novel passion for service. One was the Trinitarians, founded in Rome in 1198, the other, Our Lady of Mercy, co-established by St. Raymond of Pennafort in 1223 in Barcelona. Both orders adopted a common mission: the freeing of slaves captured by Muslims. The Trinitarians designated at least one third of all monies collected toward the freeing of captives. Members of the Order of Mercy likewise collected money to buy freedom; they also took a fourth vow. If any man could not be bought back from a slaveholder, each member pledged that he would willingly give his own life in exchange for the slave. It is estimated that from the thirteenth to the eighteenth centuries these two orders freed more than one million souls from slavery.[17] As Christ had taught, no man has greater love than to lay down his life for another.

~~~

Looking back at the Crusades, in addition to acknowledging the gifts already mentioned, the modern reader can draw two lessons. The first is a lesson in truth. The Crusades were a complex series of engagements. War among civilized peoples is always tragic, a reminder that our chief

16 Cited in John Laux, *Church History: A Complete History of the Catholic Church to the Present Day* (New York: Benziger Brothers, 1936), 317.

17 See Laux, *Church History*, 318.
~~~

enemy is the sin that divides us. For Christians, battle may at times be a duty, even a sacred one, though it is one to be taken up as a last resort. That said, we can and should be grateful that the Church encouraged men to protect Arab and other Eastern Christians; we can be grateful that the Church of the Middle Ages blocked the advance of Islamic expansion—sometimes gloriously as at the Battle of Lepanto in 1571—and preserved political freedom for the West.

The second lesson regards charity. When Jesus commanded Christians to love our enemies, he outlawed among Christian peoples any concept of a "total war." Not the least because we have no "total enemies." Christ died for all men, including the Muslim. The Church's just war tradition explains well those conditions under which lethal force is justified. These days, when Western cities are regularly targeted by Islamic terrorists, and Shiites and Sunnis are at war, a remarkable feature of contemporary Islamic life is too often overlooked: conversions. Over the past fifteen years, worldwide, researchers have found a dramatic spike among Muslims embracing Christianity, either due to the witness of some fifteen thousand active Christian missionaries in the Middle East, through rejection of mounting Muslim violence, or even direct inspirations from God or the Blessed Virgin Mary, whom Muslims already regard with reverence.[18]

---

18 See D. A. Miller and P. Johnstone, "Believers in Christ from a Muslim Background: A Global Consensus," in *Interdisciplinary Journal of Research on Religion* 11 (2015): 1–19, and D. A. Miller, "Living Among the Breakage: Contextual Theology-Making and Ex-Muslim Christians," Phd. Thesis at the University of Edinburgh (2014): 94–100.

In the final analysis, the Church does not tell good men that they must forever put down their arms. Indeed, one of the greatest needs of our time is a revival of the ideal of chivalry. Young men exploding with energy and the just pride born of strength need to see their life's work in civil society not first as the fostering of the growth of their 401k but rather the fostering of a society in which their families and others can serve God and live at peace with one another, a society, in the words of the Baltimore Catechism, in which man can know, love, and serve God in this life and be happy with him in the next. And if the Christian must sometimes defend the peace with arms, it is always with an eye to that final peace which passes all understanding.

But the assault of war was not the only crisis to besiege the medieval Church. Returning to the sixteenth century, while Islam continued to threaten Europe from without, another crisis threatened to shatter the Church from within.

7

SINNERS: THE GIFT OF ABASEMENT

"Aristotle is to theology what darkness is to light."

Martin Luther

THE year 1517 would be as traumatic as had been the fall of Rome in 410. Only, there was this difference. In the first northern invasions, it was merely the gold of Rome that the barbarians wanted; in the second northern invasion, it was her soul. Martin Luther's posting of his Ninety-Five Theses marked the beginning of the end of a unified Christian civilization in the West, the rise of nationalism among Europe's kings, and a turn away from reason toward a subjective understanding of faith. And worst of all: the disaster that ensued was partially Rome's fault.

Sometimes the conflict between the Protestant reformers of the sixteenth century and the Church is described as a clash between individual conscience and the demands of public authority. There is some truth to this description. More directly, though, what was at stake in the conflict that ensued between the Church and the "reformers," in addition to religious truth, was the value of ordered *freedom*. If the Church, during the eleventh through the thirteenth centuries, invigorated the West against Islamic armies, against Protestants, her greater contributions were at the level of culture. Thus against King Henry VIII and the other Protestant princes, the Church remained as the one supranational authority that could check the power and ambitions that secular governments held over their people; against John Calvin and the roaming mobs of Protestant iconoclasts, the popes threw their enthusiasm and their money behind the great renaissance artists such as Raphael (1483–1520) and Bernini (1598–1680); against Martin Luther's dark counsel of predestination, the Catholic humanist Erasmus argued for freedom of the will.

Purification was needed. As I hope to make clear over the next two chapters, though, by the end of the Reformation crisis, and spurred on by her own pastors, the Church displayed her never-ending capacity to act as a leaven of cultural renewal. After accepting her abasement, the Church's work of rejuvenation would begin first at home, become manifest through the arts, and be carried forward to the newly discovered ends of the world.

~~~

Protestants named a widespread discontent. By 1500, the pope, his cardinals in Rome, and many of the clergy had squandered their moral capital. "I do not know whether the princes of the Church have ever coveted the privileges of this world," wrote Erasmus in 1521, "as we see today."[1] The Church was rich and her estates had grown fat. As the good pope Leo X observed only a few years earlier: "The

---

1 Erasmus, "Letter to Jodocus," 10 May 1521 in John C. Olin, ed., *Christian Humanism and the Reformation: Selected Writings of Erasmus* (New York: Fordham University Press, 1987), 152.
~~~

lack of rule in the monasteries of France and the immodest life of the monks have come to such a pitch that neither kings nor princes, nor the faithful at large have any respect left for them."[2]

Half a century before Leo X, Pope Pius II (d. 1464) had appointed a commission of clerics known for their integrity to conduct a fact-finding study into the corruption in the Church. In the presence of this commission, Pius II announced the program of his papacy: "Two things are particularly near my heart: the war with the Turks and the reform of the Roman court." He admitted frankly, "The amendment of the whole state of ecclesiastical affairs, which I have determined to undertake, depends upon this court as its model. I propose to begin by improving the morals of ecclesiastics here, and banishing all simony and other abuses."[3] And these were the criticisms of the Church's friends.

Her enemies could be less sparing. The infamous Florentine Niccolò Machiavelli (1469–1527), author of the *Prince* and sometime advisor to two Roman pontiffs on the art of ruling, spoke this prophecy about the Church only a few years prior to Luther's public challenge.

> If the rulers of Christian lands had kept religion true to the principles set down by its founder, the states and republics of Christendom would be more united and happier than they are. But there is no better evidence of its decline than to see how the people who are closest to the Church of Rome, the center of our religion, have the least faith. Anyone examining

---

2 Cited by Will Durant in *The Story of Civilization,* vol. 6, *The Reformation* (New York: Simon and Schuster, 1957), 20.

3 Ibid., 12.

> the principles of our religion and observing how far present practice has strayed from them would doubtless conclude that ruin or severe punishment is at hand.[4]

Luther was the loudest voice, though not the only voice, crying for reform. The practices of nepotism (the sale of offices to friends), simony (the preference of office to relatives), concubinage, and the abuse of the sale of indulgences seemed more than any one pope could correct. Indeed, some popes had been part of the problem.

During Luther's time, the wittiest attacks upon the clergy came neither from popes nor proto-protestants but from the Dutch Humanist, and loyal Catholic, Desiderius Erasmus (1466–1536). His *Praise of Folly*, for one, written in 1509 during a stay in England with his friend Sir Thomas More, is a hilarious satire. In it he pokes fun at the vices of the Church and her clergy with the serious aim of encouraging a renewal of morals. Especially targeted are the theologians. He mocks their character. Erasmus's fictional spokeswoman, Folly, calls the theologians of his day a "supercilious and touchy" lot who are ready to denounce anyone who makes jest of their work "as a heretic on the spot." He satirizes their questions. "Could God have taken on the form of a woman, a devil, a donkey, a gourd or a flint stone? If so, how could a gourd have preached sermons?" He derides their maxims. "Better to let the whole world perish down to the last crumb and stitch, as they say, than to tell a single tiny insignificant lie."[5]

---

4 Machiavelli, *Discourses*, trans. Donno, 1.12.

5 Erasmus, *Praise of Folly*, trans. Radice, 152–56.

Of course, all this rollicking wit was delivered prior to the outbreak of the actual Reformation. In the early days of Luther's career, Erasmus even hoped, like other Catholics, for his success; "in the beginning Luther had as much approbation on all sides as, I believe, has come to any mortal for several centuries past."[6] The Church had indeed grown fat, and everyone knew it. What quickly became manifest, however, was that Luther desired far more than rejuvenation. He wanted revolution. He wanted an entirely new church for which he would be the chief spokesman.

~~~

Martin Luther was the son of a miner and suffered a brutal childhood. Biographies stress the unhappiness of his early years as a possible explanation for his later mental instability. Certainly, his parents beat him severely. He entered religious life, in the first instance, to escape the tyranny of his mother and father; by his own account, "it was this harshness and severity of the life I led with them that forced me subsequently to run away to a monastery and become a monk."[7] Unfortunately, even once he took the habit inside the walls of the Augustinian monastery at Efurt, he never found peace in his religion. He was haunted by his own sense of wretchedness. He refused to believe that his sins were forgiven, and later, as a priest, he was terrified of saying the Mass. Such thoughts clouded his mind until one day, as he tells us, somewhere during 1508 and

6 Erasmus, "Letter to Jodocus," 152.

7 Cited in Henry Ganss, "Martin Luther," in *The Catholic Encyclopedia* (1910).
~~~

1509, he received a revelation. As he put it in an early manifesto, he realized how it was that "Faith alone" can save; this act, and this act alone "is the saving and efficacious use of the Word of God."[8] Works avail nothing. The priesthood offers no help. Confessions confuse. Church traditions mostly obscure.

Luther's new found "liberty" was to free men from fifteen centuries of doctrine, development, councils, and philosophy. In an early dispute, he pronounced, for instance, "In vain does one fashion a logic of faith."[9] True, Luther was at heart a pamphleteer. (The work of systematizing his ideas would be left to later disciples, like Melanchthon.) Yet how far from the Catholic spirit had he already roamed! Far from displacing reason by faith, his favorite Church father, St. Augustine, had worked tirelessly to show their common source. In the Augustinian tradition, revelation and reason did not vie in a zero sum competition. Rather, as Augustine wrote in one of his most widely read works in the Middle Ages, *On Christian Teaching*, "Logic permeates the whole body of Scripture, rather like a network of muscles."[10] For Luther, it was otherwise. Alas, after his personal insight, such passages could not move the young monk. To him, none of the Church's natural aids (for example, reason) nor her supernatural prompts (for example, sacraments) register on the scale when weighed against the individual's private, inward, and privately verified experience of faith.

---

8 Luther, *Freedom of a Christian*, ed. Dillenberger, 55.

9 Luther, *Disputation Against Scholastic Theology*, eds. Lull and Russell, prop. 46.

10 St. Augustine, *On Christian Teaching*, trans. Green, 2.143.

The consequences of this turn were soon felt. Early in Luther's reforming career, a duke had invited him to preach to his people in Dresden. Upon hearing Luther expound his doctrine of faith alone, the duke warned the young friar against following this line of reasoning, for it "would only make the people presumptuous and mutinous."[11] This is just what happened. In the immediate aftermath, between 1524 and 1526, Luther's preaching helped ignite one of the bloodiest peasant revolts witnessed in European history. One estimate puts the number of dead at 130,000, far more than the number of American soldiers killed during the Korean, Vietnam, Afghanistan, and Iraq wars combined. Once the revolt was underway, Luther did not like what he saw. In one of his more subtle works, *Against the Murdering, Thieving Hordes of Peasants*, he sought ruthlessly to suppress the revolution calling on princes to "brandish their swords, to free, save, help and pity the poor people forced to join the peasants—but the wicked, smite, stab and slay all you can." The bloodshed that Luther's preaching encouraged was appalling. Luther came from peasant stock. He knew their hardships. Yet when the killings reached his ears, as for example when a band of peasants to the sound of music speared the Count of Helfenstein to death in the presence of his wife and child, Luther rode throughout Germany trying to undo the fury that his words helped to unleash. To the beleaguered aristocrats he therefore counseled, "The times are so extraordinary that a prince can win heaven more easily by bloodshed than by prayer."[12] Almost

---

11 Durant, *The Story of Civilization*, 6:345.

12 Cited in Owen Chadwick, *The Penguin History of the Reformation of the Church* (London: Penguin, 1990), 60.

as quickly, Luther's fire ignited a second revolution, this time among his fellow preachers; it would be a revolution that Luther would have no power to stop.

Luther's doctrine of faith alone isolated Christian belief from reason and separated private conviction from public authorities. Not surprisingly, his revolutionary teaching soon began to eat up the revolutionaries. Other reformers took up Luther's cry. Disagreement multiplied, and faction led to faction. Thus the Swiss priest Ulrich Zwingli (1484–1531) decided he, too, could throw off the yoke of his bishop's authority. His first act of insurrection was liturgical. In 1519, Zwingli resolved to begin preaching not from the lectionary but from his own uniquely designed schedule of New Testament texts. Brazen liturgical innovation was here the first step along the march toward outright heresy.

Zwingli's decisive break came a few years later. In 1523, this Swiss "Luther" convened two debates between himself and another priest. The men argued, then Zwingli called for a vote. Those who had gathered for the debate cast their lots in favor of Zwingli's side. Zwingli regarded this positive count as an authorization equivalent to the approval of an ecumenical council. The sacraments, he and his followers proclaimed, were merely symbols. There is nothing mystical about the true Supper of the Mass; it is but an expression of fellowship, and "the bread," as one of Zwingli's Anabaptist disciples would put it, "is naught but bread."[13] This, in turn, enraged Luther. The two reformers

---

[13] Conrad Grebel (an early disciple of Zwingli and one of the first Anabaptists), "Letter to Thomas Müntzer," 5 September 1524 in Hillerbrand, ed., *The Protestant Reformation* (London: Macmillan, 1968), 125.

tried to reconcile their views. After talks broke down, Luther denounced the Swiss reformer as a heretic and quipped, "I would rather drink blood with the papists than mere wine with the Zwinglians."[14] Besides being a good debater, Zwingli was also a zealous general. To enforce his newly minted orthodoxy, Zwingli led a local militia of his followers in military campaigns against his Catholic neighbors, eventually dying on the battlefield in 1531.

The wheel of revolution would turn yet again. Zwingli, like Luther, wanted a Protestant state. Not everyone agreed. Zwingli's use of violence led other revolutionaries to break in another direction, dissatisfied that the Swiss reformer had not gone far enough in his interpretations of Scripture. Thus were born the Anabaptists. These Protestants accepted Luther's appeal to Scripture alone and adopted Zwingli's rejection of the sacraments but affixed their own personal stamp: non-violence and a ban on infant baptism. More revolutionary bloodshed followed when in 1535 King Henry VIII took off Thomas More's head and in 1555 Calvin knocked down all the statues of Geneva.

~~~

In Catholic teaching, the Church is not a club for the spiritually elite. The Church is the ark of salvation. She is the divinely ordained means by which the wreck of sinful humanity is carried over the raging storms of time into the Father's house. She exists in three modalities: the Church triumphant, the Church suffering, and the Church militant.

---

[14] Cited in Crocker, *Triumph: The Power and the Glory of the Catholic Church* (New York: Crown Forum, 2003), 250.
~~~

The Church triumphant experiences even now the joys of heaven; members of the Church suffering endure their final purification in purgatory, while the rest of us—we who walk upon the earth—wage a mortal conflict for our souls and the souls of our fellows. It is the necessity of this earthly struggle, in which moral calamities as much as triumphs of grace are still possible, that has kept the Church from identifying herself as a sect, or as a haven for the "pure." This teaching is radical. This teaching is often mocked. And it is based on the words of Christ. As Jesus warned his disciples, in this age, both the good and the bad must grow up together. Judgment in the Church must be mixed with mercy, and be circumspect. Only in the last day will hearts be revealed and all accounts settled.

There is another reason the Church can never produce a perfect society. An overly zealous ardor for purity within the flock would cause more harm than good. Religion, like any human passion, can be harnessed for both good and evil ends. And yet people tend to forget that the great calamities of the past century, the bloodiest century of all recorded centuries, with its World Wars, its genocides, its gulags, were the product not of religion but of messianic materialism. Karl Marx (1818–83) was modernity's first prophet without God. He preached Christianity without Christ and, through his revolution, tried to drag the New Jerusalem down to earth. What the Marxists and the revolutionary materialists of our time preach is a false religion. To aim for a perfect society would be to ruin the world. As Pope Benedict recently reflected in *Spe Salvi* (*Saved in Hope*), possibly his greatest encyclical:

> Anyone who promises a better world that is guaranteed to last for ever is making a false promise; he is overlooking human freedom. Freedom must constantly be won over for the cause of good. Free assent to the good never exists simply by itself. If there were structures which could irrevocably guarantee a determined—good—state of the world, man's freedom would be denied, and hence they would not be good structures at all.[15]

In other words, weeds must be allowed to grow up alongside the good seed. When judging the Church of the Renaissance, the Reformation, or any era, we must therefore proceed with this principle in mind. The Church strives for purity. The Church never aims to uproot all evil either in the world or among the faithful. As her Lord cautioned, "Lest in gathering the weeds you root up the wheat along with them. Let both grow together until the harvest" (Mt 13:29–30). Our Lord did not counsel lawlessness. Jesus did establish, however, a fellowship that would ever remain open to sinners even while it aimed to transform them into saints. When Christ formed the Church, he constituted a field hospital as much as a regiment. It was a dangerous teaching. This preference for mercy, this delicate balance between law and freedom, made the Church prey to abuse by the unscrupulous and open to attacks by the rigid.

The scars have never fully healed. Though Calvin's death marks the end of the period of the magisterial (teaching) Protestant reformers, the principle of division has continued unabated. From these four primal breaks (Luther's in Germany, Zwingli's in Switzerland, Calvin's in France, King Henry's in England), the wide family of Protestant

---

[15] Benedict XVI, *Spe Salvi* (2007), 25.

denominations has grown. Today there exist some thirty-five thousand separate denominations, with one new one added every second day.[16]

Since the last council, Catholics and Protestants alike have been working to repair wounds inflicted over the Reformation. As Pope St. John Paul II put it, the Church has set herself "irrevocably" toward the path of unity.[17] This is all for the good. Today a conservative Evangelical and an orthodox Roman Catholic are likely to find more agreement among themselves on moral issues—the evil of abortion or the definition of marriage if not yet on issues such as the nature of the Church—than they will find with socially-progressive and heterodox members of their own communions. I wonder when Sir Thomas More, looking out from the Tower of London, or William Tyndale, as he prepared to die by the hands of the Inquisition, would have imagined the future reconciliation of Christians to come about. If such a question was not commonly asked in the sixteenth century, it is all but impossible to ignore in the twenty-first century. After the birth of militant secularism, the return of martyrdoms in the twentieth century, and the rise of ecumenism, many intelligent responses have come from both sides of the Catholic and Protestant divide. The Anglican apologist C. S. Lewis claimed no knowledge as to when reconciliation might come. But he did suggest a method. In his correspondence with an Italian priest, Fr. Giovanni Calabria, Lewis proposed that "united action,

---

16 This figure based on Barett, *World Christian Encyclopedia* (Oxford: Oxford University Press, 2001), 1:10, 1:5—a monumental work of Protestant scholarship.

17 John Paul II, *Ut unum sint* (1995), 3.

prayer, fortitude and (should God so will) united deaths for Christ" would likely be God's instruments for reuniting a divided Christendom. "By doing the truth which we already know," Lewis concluded, "let us make progress towards the truth which as yet we are ignorant of. Then, without doubt, we shall be one: for truth is one."[18] Amen and amen.

During the sixteenth century, the Church paid a heavy price for her sins, real, exaggerated, and imagined. And yet her true reformation was still to come.

---

[18] C. S. Lewis, letter 5 to Fr. Giovanni Calabria, in *The Latin Letters of C. S. Lewis* (South Bend, IN: St. Augustine Press, 1998), 43.

8

REFORMERS: THE GIFT OF RENEWAL

"What if I should do what St. Francis did?"

St. Ignatius of Loyola

IN response to the cries of Luther, Calvin, Zwingli, and Henry, the Church answered with a three-pronged counter thrust: the Council of Trent, Baroque art, and the mission of the Jesuits. Confidence had been shaken. The first reply, and the one that all others relied upon, was a steadying of doctrine and internal discipline. Vast regions in Germany, parts of France, and all of England were claiming independence from the papacy. Amidst several false starts, and after overcoming the opposition of both the French King and the Holy Roman emperor, the pope finally convened his long-awaited general council in a small city nestled within the Alps at the borders of Switzerland, Austria, and Italy named Trent.

The council's three sessions, conducted between 1545 and 1563, updated the edifice of Catholic teaching and internal structure. Most pressing was the reform of the clergy. Absentee bishops, the sale of Church offices, and the housing of mistresses were among the more notable practices the bishops set out to curb. It wasn't easy. Priests weren't used to taking popes seriously. It is perhaps telling that by this time no pope had been canonized for three hundred years. Pope Paul IV (r. 1555–59) was probably the first bishop of Rome able to take effective action. He came from a military background and executed his policies like a general. To catch vagrant monks, for instance, whose brown cloaks served as a cover for indiscretion, the pope imposed in the city of Rome a soft form of martial law in 1558. All monks were to return to their monasteries by sundown. Paul IV ordered the gates of Rome closed. Night fell. Soldiers were sent, like anxious hounds, to scour the streets. Those monks who remained on the street were rounded up and tossed into jail.[1] Such was the man who oversaw some of the earliest work of the council.

The cleric who did the most to implement the council's reforms was not, however, a pope but the archbishop of Milan, St. Charles Borromeo (1538–84). Charles was born into powerful circles. His mother was a Medici, his uncle, the future Pope Pius IV. He was intelligent and driven; his personal holiness was legendary. He earned a doctorate in civil and canon law from the University of Paris in 1559, the same year that his uncle appointed him to the position of papal secretary of state. Thus, at the age of twenty-four, at the time of life when some young men today are still playing video games, Charles organized an ecumenical council and attended its third session (1562–63). All this is to his credit; but his greatest work was still to come. Like Cardinal Wojtyla did after Vatican II, Borromeo set to work

---

1 This episode reported in Durant, *The Story of Civilization*, 6:899.

implementing both the spirit and the letter of the council's reforms first in his own home.

One of his first tasks was to call a local synod and gather his 1,200 clergy. It was with his brethren that he began his grand work. He made endless visitations to the city's sick; on 11 November 1564, he opened a new seminary with three Jesuits at its head. He narrowly escaped an assassination attempt in 1569 and refused to leave his flock in Milan when a plague broke out a few years later. For all these deeds, Charles was loved. While the years immediately after the Reformation demanded a renewal of Church discipline, perhaps the council's more lasting work was its solidification of her doctrine.

What did Trent decree? At the beginning of the council, effort was made to seek common ground with the reformers. Leading Protestants, among them Luther's highly erudite disciple Melanchthon (1497–1560), were asked to submit statements on doctrines like justification and even invited to attend sessions. The effort soon proved fruitless. Hope for reconciliation broke after the Lutherans declined to accept the real presence in the Eucharist; and besides, irreconcilable conflicts already separated Protestants from among each other. Unity between Catholics and Protestants would not be recovered.

Two options lay before the bishops. One was a policy of accommodation. Another was a more vigorous defense and development of existing doctrine, in other words, a more vigorous defense and articulation of the treasury of the apostolic tradition. The bishops chose the second course. Instead of suggesting muddied modifications that might have kept more of the Protestants within the flock (a strategy certain princes proposed), the council produced a series of stunning affirmations of traditional teaching. At almost every turn, their declarations refuted the claims of the reformers. For instance, at the level of doctrine, where Luther reduced the source of Christian belief to the Bible, Trent proclaimed that God's word spoke through both Scripture and Tradition; where Zwingli and the Anabaptists proposed a cosmos drained of sacraments, Trent reaffirmed all seven; finally, at the level of culture, where Calvin slashed paintings, the Church proclaimed the goodness of the sensual in worship. As the council rather laconically stated, no doubt with John Calvin in mind, "If anyone says that the ceremonies, vestments, and outward signs which the Catholic Church uses in the celebration of masses, are incentives to impiety rather than stimulants to piety, let him be anathema" (canon 7, session 22).[2]

That blessing was all that artists needed to hear. The Church's affirmation of the artist's work within the drama of salvation would give rise to a new form of artistic expression: the Baroque.

~~~

What defines Baroque art is its exaltation of glory. God has visited the earth: the things of the earth, therefore, ought to lift us to the glories of heaven. Baroque architecture, like its painting and music, revels in the materiality of things; it displays the splendor of sense to give joy to the spirit.

---

2 *The Canons and Decrees of the Council of Trent*, trans. H. J. Schroeder, 152.
~~~

It is surely a paradox. How marvelous it is that the very moment when scandal had sunk the Church into her lowest condition she should give birth to the most exuberant expression of the arts ever known to Europe or any other civilization. Yet that is what she did. In this period, between roughly 1550 and 1650, nearly all of the greatest artists were devout. Bernini (1598–1680) often attended spiritual retreats and the exercises of St. Ignatius of Loyola; Peter Paul Rubens (1577–1640) began painting each day only after hearing Mass.[3] In the field of architecture, for a hundred years after the Reformation, virtually no new churches were built in England. During this same period in the Catholic countries, a new style of architecture burst forth, beginning with *Il Gesu* in Rome (1584). If Romanesque architecture, with its solid masses, was ideally suited to depict the immanence of God, and if Gothic architecture, with its climbing arches, spoke majestically of God's transcendence, Baroque architecture depicted the Mass as a drama. The seventeenth century depicted the sacraments through a divinely choreographed play of movement and of light.

Rome, of course, remains the world's capital for Baroque architecture. (Vilnius, the capital city of Lithuania, is the second.) It is fitting that the first building in the new style should be in Rome, should be a church, and should be the home to an industrious new religious order. Surpassing the influence even of the Benedictines and the Dominicans, the Counter-Reformation's first religious congregation would

---

3 An observation made by Kenneth Clark in *Civilisation: A Personal View* (New York: Harper and Row, 1969), 175.

win back much of what the Church had lost in the Reformation, and more. Besides ferment in government and the arts, the later part of the Catholic sixteenth century was also an era of mystics and reformers. At the same moment that Teresa of Avila was restoring discipline among her Carmelite sisters, John of the Cross sat in prison penning his *Dark Night of the Soul*, Philip Neri in Rome—father of the Oratorians—took families on picnics and told jokes, and Francis de Sales was developing a spirituality suited especially for the laity. It is perhaps fitting though that in that rough age of spiritual giants, the one order whose work would outshine the others was founded by a soldier.

~~~

The third point of the spear, so to speak, in the Church's counter thrust was headed by Ignatius of Loyola. The year 1521 was portentous. In that year, four after Luther pinned up his Ninety-Five Theses, the pope finally, and reluctantly, answered with his bull of excommunication. That same year, a young Spanish noble was hit by a cannon ball. Iñigo of Loyola (1491–1556) served in the army of the Spanish crown. He was defending the city of Pamplona, the ancient capital of the Kingdom of Navarre at the northern edge of Spain, against a French militia when iron tore through his legs.

Ignatius had been a worldly soldier. His lengthy convalescence forced him to reconsider his aims. He loved romantic literature, and so asked to have some that he might pass the time. The castle where he was convalescing had few of them. His attendant brought him what they had.
~~~

It was a copy of *The Life of Christ* by Ludoph of Saxony, a fourteenth-century Carthusian writer, as well as some lives of the saints. This was not what the soldier had in mind. But reading of the first martyrs and great heroes of the Church, such as Benedict, Augustine, and the famed monk Antony, fired his imagination. It is not that the young man gave up ambition. It is that his aspirations turned to loftier aims: to the conquest of the world for Christ and the renewal of all things for the greater glory of God. In third person prose, he records the movement of his thoughts this way.

> In the meantime the divine mercy was at work substituting for these thoughts others suggested by his recent readings. While perusing the life of Our Lord and the saints, he began to reflect, saying to himself: "What if I should do what St. Francis did?" "What if I should act like St. Dominic?" He pondered over these things in his mind, and kept continually proposing to himself serious and difficult things. He seemed to feel a certain readiness for doing them, with no other reason except this thought: "St. Dominic did this; I, too, will do it." "St. Francis did this; therefore I will do it." These heroic resolutions remained for a time, and then other vain and worldly thoughts followed. This succession of thoughts occupied him for a long while, those about God alternating with those about the world. But in these thoughts there was this difference. When he thought of worldly things it gave him great pleasure, but afterward he found himself dry and sad. But when he thought of journeying to Jerusalem, and of living only on herbs, and practicing austerities, he found pleasure not only while thinking of them, but also when he had ceased.[4]

Imagination gave way to resolution. On his bed, Ignatius determined that, henceforth, he should live no longer for

---

[4] St. Ignatius, *The Autobiography of St. Ignatius of Loyola*, ed. J. F. X. O'Connor, 16.

the glory of arms and for women; he should labor no more for the esteem of the great and the powerful among men, but only for God. That would be his congregation's new catchphrase: *Ad maiorem Dei gloriam*. These words still echo in the chests of noble men and mark the letterhead of hundreds of Jesuit colleges and universities around the globe. By this time, Ignatius was middle-aged. After his leg healed, he did what other men of his rank and temperament would have been too proud to consider, or too afraid to attempt. He went back to school. He enrolled in Latin classes alongside young boys, and afterward, at the age of thirty-seven, found himself mulling over Aristotle and memorizing propositions from St. Thomas at the University of Paris. It is there that he found a group of friends who would join him in his mission.

Students were attracted by Ignatius's sober zeal. He lived as a man conscious of his mission. When someone would promise to do something in a week or in two weeks' time, for instance, Ignatius would often reply, "How is that? Do you think you are going to live that long?"[5] Others gathered around him for direction. This experience would later form the basis of the famed *Spiritual Exercises*, a sequence of meditations that evoke scenes from the life of Christ in order to stir pious resolutions.

Just as he had found God through the inspired promptings of the imagination during his forced convalescence, so he would lead others to do the same. The men prayed together. Some of them even bound themselves to the traditional promises of poverty, chastity, and obedience and

[5] St. Ignatius, *The Autobiography*, 5.

added a fourth: the companions of Jesus would follow the pope unreservedly. Liberty in the imagination did not translate for Ignatius to independence from authority. His was to be an active order, not bound to convents, nor to habits, but prepared, like a specialized militia, to drop into any theatre of conflict to which the Holy Father called. And they answered. Through this tiny band of brothers, the Church would evangelize much of the known world.

~~~

Every age produces its own crises. And, by grace, God raises in every age men and women sufficient for the times. In the early centuries of the Church, it was the Benedictines who civilized Europe through their agriculture, their liturgy, and their manuscripts. In the High Middle Ages, it was the Franciscans who restored lady poverty to her pride of place, just as it was the Dominicans who kept lady philosophy from abandoning the schools. In the modern era, the greatest teachers were the Jesuits. The rate of growth of their schools was phenomenal. By the time of Ignatius's death, the Jesuits operated some 33 schools in Sicily, Italy, Spain, Portugal, Austria, Bohemia, Germany, and France. By the close of the sixteenth century, that number had risen to 245, and nearly doubled again by 1625. By the time of Pope Clement XIV's unfortunate suppression of the order in 1773, the Jesuits operated 546 schools in Europe and 123 in missionary territories around the globe. By the time of Mozart and the Boston Tea Party, the Jesuits had established themselves literally as the educators of Europe.
~~~

What moved them to invest so heavily? Non-believers often look with suspicion upon Christian charity. Certainly, the order gained recruits from their schools. But mercantile motives hardly account for the sacrifice that generations of Europe's brightest men made of their lives at home and abroad. The best evidence for the generosity of their ambition—and for their success in shaping talent—is seen from the sorts of men of culture that their system produced. The eighteenth century was an age of dazzling wit. What was brilliant about the era could not have been conceived apart from the Jesuits's fertile labor in the field of European education. Whatever gifts of culture were imparted by the likes of Descartes the philosopher and mathematician, Bossuet the preacher to the French royal court, Molière the comedic playwright, Calderón de la Barca the Spanish poet, and even Voltaire the skeptic—to say nothing of the literary and spiritual formation of countless lesser known scientists, politicians, and peasants—for one and half centuries was in some measure the fruit of the academies of the Jesuits. It should not surprise that some eighty countries of the world have published commemorative stamps honoring one or more Jesuit for his contribution to the development of their national culture.[6]

And system it was. Beyond the academies, the order also produced the greatest single document on the practice of teaching: the *Ratio Studiorum*. The Jesuit *Plan of Studies* was published in 1599 after years of consultation and the scrutiny of the best insights of medieval and renaissance

---

6 Fairfield University hosts a fascinating website titled "A Philatelic Display of the Jesuit Mission," which describes each Jesuit so honored by a national stamp; see faculty.fairfield.edu/jmac/sj/sjscienti.htm.

educational theorists. In it the authors provided a flexible template for a classical education suited for an age of scientific advancement and political expansion. Though the work of the order was temporarily suspended for forty-one years, the lessons learned in the art of teaching were not lost. Pope Pius VII restored the order in 1814.[7] It took just over a century for the Jesuits to regain the membership they had at the time of the suppression. From 1930 to 1960, however, their growth in colleges exceeded even their original achievement. According to official records, at the eve of the Second Vatican Council, Jesuits ran over 4,000 schools: 1,009 in Africa, 1,379 in Asia and Oceania, 602 in Europe, 378 in South America, and 691 in Canada and the United States.[8]

But that is to anticipate. In the early modern era, besides schools, Jesuits provided Europe with its first astronomers; abroad, as explorers discovered America and the Far East, it was the Jesuits, above all, who did most to ferry the message of the Gospel across oceans and rivers. At the end of Ignatius's life, his order had one thousand members scattered throughout one hundred houses. When Ignatius's greatest collaborator, St. Francis Xavier, died off the coast

---

7 Some work did carry on. Five schools in Russia, a few in Sicily and France, and one in America were in operation by the pope's reinstatement. Most notably, in the United States, Bishop John Carroll founded in 1789 America's first Catholic college in Georgetown. Though Carroll was a Jesuit, the order did not acquire full responsibility for the foundation till 1805.

8 For statistics, see Allan P. Farrell's introduction to his translation of the *Ratio Studiorum* (Washington, D.C.: Conference of Major Superiors of Jesuits, 1970), ii–vi.

of China, several hundred thousand East Indians, Japanese, and islanders of the Far East bore the name of Christ.

By the end of the eighteenth century, the Church had recovered from the civil and religious wars spawned by the Protestant Reformation. Through Trent, she had renewed her internal discipline, through the Baroque, she had bequeathed to the West a new and vigorous expression of beauty, and through the Jesuits, she had adapted the crusading fever and scholastic zeal of the Middle Ages to the conditions of newly expanding continents. Even as persecutions threatened to extinguish Catholicism in the Old World, missionaries would transmit the faith to men and women of the New.

9

MISSIONARIES: THE GIFT FOR A NEW WORLD

"The Huron language will be your St. Thomas and your Aristotle."

St. Jean de Brébeuf

DURING the sixteenth through the nineteenth centuries, alongside the scientific, industrial, and republican revolutions at home, European explorers brought the Faith into contact with peoples untouched by the history of the Jews or the civilization once united by Greek literature and Roman arms. Not since the time of the Apostle Paul had the Church experienced an era of greater expansion. Whole continents were won. Outside of Europe, the losses inflicted by the Protestant Reformation and the French Revolution were amply compensated by the victories of missionaries abroad. These new Christians understood well the great treasure that the missionaries brought; many among both the gift-givers and the gift-receivers paid for the privilege of the Faith in the currency of their blood. The Church's universal calendar of saints offers homage to these new believers. Some heroes are commemorated by name, such as St. Charles Lwanga and the companions of Uganda (Feast, 3 June), St. Paul Miki and the twenty-six martyrs of Japan (Feast, 6 February), and St. Kateri Tekakwitha of North America, the "Lily of the Mohawks" (Feast, 14 July). While these gains in the worldwide missions brought new glory to God, and carried some of the gifts of European civilization to distant shores, the West's "discovery" also raised novel questions about the creed.

Christianity had been an international movement from the start. Since the Church's official welcome of Gentiles at the Council of Jerusalem (Acts 15), all men, in principle, could find embrace in the arms of Christ's Body. By the early modern era, for centuries already the Catholic Church had been, you might say, a sort of model United Nations. Whatever notional unity the United Nations aspires to in our time had long ago been realized at the level of faith and culture by the Roman Catholic Church. First Jew, then Arab, then Indian, Egyptian, Greek, Roman, African, Gaul, German, Saxon, and more were welcomed into her family. All this is obvious to the historian. At the time, it was not always clear to individual Christians. The accidents of war and migration had, by the late Middle Ages, concentrated much of Christianity on European soil and, for some, obscured this truth of the Church's deep catholicity

In the early modern era, Europe encountered "untouched" peoples. How was she to treat them? As the seventeenth and eighteenth centuries rolled forward, the Church's greatest obstacle to her evangelical mission was not alien powers but Christian princes and their colonists. In tracing the gifts of the Church, arguably, her most lasting contribution in the era of the missions was to proclaim the dignity of slaves and the universal solidarity among peoples.

~~~

Since the eighteenth century, the legend of the noble savage has circulated within the West. Rousseau and Marx were earlier adherents to the theory, but countless painters, politicians, and singers have followed in their tread. The story is simple, and in rough outline may be described as follows: Prior to civilization, prior to cities, prior to marriage and maybe religion, man lived in perfect harmony with man. Therefore, if you wish to create a perfect society, you must return man to his "natural" conditions. Remove religion, dissolve marriage, recover the countryside, then violence, oppression, and war will cease. Empirical evidence of course has never supported the myth. Nevertheless, for those who reject the Bible, the myth has served as a substitute for the Genesis account of Adam's fall. And for those who loathe Christianity, the myth justifies, in their own minds at least, their anger at the arrival of missionaries.

Five millennia ago, whatever the rain forests might have looked like for Cro-Magnon man, by the time history began to be set down, men regarded conflict as being as permanent as the seasons. The Roman proverb *Si vis pacem para bellum* sums up the wisdom of pagan antiquity: "If you want peace, prepare for war." By the time of St. Paul's first mission to the Gentiles, the will to oppression is already an old habit. Consider but one practice. Christianity was born into a world that regarded slavery as a fact as permanent as war. In his letter to Philemon, for instance, St. Paul does not concern himself with the evil of the institution but with the implications of Baptism. Onesimus was a runaway slave. He had heard Paul's preaching, been baptized, and
~~~

was now a friend to the Apostle. The Apostle was to send Onesimus back to his master. At this time in the Roman Empire, there were more slaves than freemen. Roman law decreed runaway slaves liable to capital punishment. According to the standing custom, Philemon, the master, could have justly put Onesimus to death. Onesimus may have even stolen property. Whatever the case, St. Paul tells Philemon to "charge that to my account" (Phlm 18).

Paul's gesture of reconciliation put into circulation a new currency. Without bothering to challenge Roman law directly, Paul calls this slave his friend, his brother in Christ, and thus undermines, before the slave's owner, the brutal logic of the institution. The first premise was now missing: before oppressor and oppressed, before master and slave, there now rests a more solid solidarity, a friendship between men born of a new human nature, one rooted in the new Adam, Jesus Christ. Philemon, like Onesimus, was a Christian; each was indebted to Paul; both were brothers in Christ. "Accordingly, though I am bold enough in Christ to command you to do what is required, yet for love's sake I prefer to appeal to you" (Phlm 8–9). The old pattern of strong over weak had been transformed. A higher law, the law of Christ, had risen in the hearts of men and was destined to scatter the darkness that bound them.

In the first centuries, the Church did not so much as oppose slavery as undermine its conditions. Believers created a society within Roman society. Slave and master shared the same sacraments, were buried in the same tombs, and could rise to the same ecclesiastical offices. St. Jerome mentions how clerics of servile origin were not uncommon[1]—indeed, by the third century, at least two former slaves, Pius and Callistus, had risen to the office of the papacy. Roman law at this time did not recognize the marriage of slaves. A father had no legal authority over his children and a mother had no protection against predators. By contrast, Church legislation insisted on the validity of a slave's marriage. In one of his homilies, St. John Chrysostom, for one, declares, "He who has immoral relations with the wife of a slave is as culpable as he who has the like relations with the wife of the prince: both are adulterers, for it is not the condition of the parties that makes the crime."[2] And yet, it is true, slavery in some forms continued for several centuries and would, at later moments in the West, be revived. The Church, in the beginning, did not see fit to launch a moral crusade against slavery the way it did, for example, against abortion.[3] Why not? Looking around him at the unbroken record of man's cruelty to man, even St. Augustine, a visionary political theorist, could sound fatalistic. After the fall, slavery looked like a permanent fixture. "It is clear, then," he mused, "that sin is the primary cause of servitude in the sense of a social status in which one man is compelled to be subjected to another man."[4]

---

1 Cf. St. Jerome, *Letter*, 82.6.

2 See citation given in P. Allard, "Slavery and Christianity," in *The Catholic Encyclopedia* (1912).

3 Compare, for instance, the first-century *Didache's* absolute condemnation of abortion with its exhortation to slaves to obey masters and masters to treat slaves well.

4 St. Augustine, *City of God*, 19.5.

In any case, over the course of centuries, councils, and frequent condemnations, the leaven took effect.[5] The unimaginable happened. Around the end of the tenth century, slavery functionally ceased to operate within Christian territories. It was only along the coastal cities, or sometimes as an act of retribution against warring Muslims in Spain, that anything like a slave market existed. During this period, our word *slave* no longer provides an easy equivalent for the term *servus*. A new political and economic designation began to appear: that of the serf (*servus*). The shift was monumental. The serf was a man bound to the land of his lord. By the twelfth century, land was plentiful but labor was scarce, as was security. By pledging himself to his lord, the serf and his family secured rights to the land and, beyond a set rent, a share in excess profits; in turn, he could count on protection from raiders. Within Christendom, the serf and the lord's exchange of arms for land rendered slavery economically obsolete.

~~~

The situation outside of Christendom was more complex. Columbus's discovery in 1492 and Hernan Cortes's arrival in Mexico in 1519 brought the Spanish Empire to the shores of the new world. Economic opportunity and prestige motivated. At the discovery of untouched peoples, Europeans during the Age of Discovery were filled with a zeal for gold, but some among them were filled with a zeal of a different sort; they were zealous for souls. Perhaps Rousseau could regard non-Europeans as sinless because

5 For discussion, see Allard, "Christianity and Slavery."
~~~

he never traveled. What the first generation of European explorers discovered among the Native Americans was a blend of innocence and savagery. Human sacrifice had virtually ceased on the European continent before the birth of Christ. When Cortes met the Aztecs, he discovered a people enslaved to dark rituals. Some historians reckon that the Aztecs delivered 20,000 bodies in their yearly offerings. That number may, in fact, be a gross underestimate given that an early chronicle at the height of Aztec power, around 1487, records that, over a four-day period, 80,400 captives were ritually killed at the Great Temple of Tenochtitlan, not far from where Our Lady would shortly appear.[6]

Ritualized sacrifice among the Aztecs served a double function. The killing and flaying of human corpses, the extracting of the victim's heart, and the thumping melodies that accompanied the grisly slaughters were tributes to their gods. The sacrifices also aimed to publicize. I offer one anecdote left from the early chronicler, Father Diego Durán. He was a sympathetic and detailed historian and recorded the stories and customs of the Indians from natives who lived prior to the conquest in his 1581 work *The History of the Indies of New Spain.* After the Aztecs defeated another people, the Huaxtec nation, the victors beckoned

---

6 This figure recorded in 1581 by Fray Diego Durán in *The History of the Indies of New Spain*, trans. with introduction by Doris Heyden (London: University of Oklahoma Press, 1994), chapter 44, pages 337-39. After his detailed account he records his own near disbelief: "All of this seemed so incredible to me that if the [records] had not forced me to put it down, and if I had not found confirmation of it in other written and painted manuscripts, I would not dare to write these things" (p. 339).

nobles and common people of the surrounding countryside to celebrate with them during a festival. The date for the festival was to coincide with the beginning of the month called *Tlacaxipehualiztli*, which means "Flaying of Men." A temple had just been completed, as had a table that was to act as an altar of sacrifice. The guests arrived. Music, gifts, and large quantities of food were poured out upon the visitors. Once all had had their fill, the male Huaxtec prisoners of war were brought forward and made to dance. These unfortunate men had been smeared with chalk, their heads matted with down, and feathers tied to their hair. Their eyelids were blackened, and a circle around their mouths was painted in red. Then the men who served in the temples arrived, each one "disguised as a god." An elaborate choreographed duel was enacted between the victim and the grim reapers of the temple. The captive was tied down and given feathered weapons and made to defend himself against an attacker. The crowd watched in rapt gaze. At the first appearance of a wound on the unfortunate man, the climax began to unfold. The chronicle records:

> Four priests, their bodies painted black, with long braided hair, dressed in garments like chasubles, ascended the stone and laid the wounded man on his back, holding him down by the feet and hands. The high priest then rose from his seat, went to the stone, and opened the chest of the victim with the knife. He took out the heart and offered the vapor that rose from it to the sun. As soon as the heart had cooled, he delivered it to the priest.

The ritual would be repeated till all the prisoners were dispatched. The next day, similar rewards were meted out, upon both the guests and the captives; this time it would not be the beating heart that was removed but the skin from the fallen warriors. The historian records the effect of the festivities on the neighboring tribes. The visiting lords returned home "bewildered"; what they saw filled them with "fright."[7] To be sure.

The Spanish conquest would put an end to such barbarism; if that be cultural imperialism, so be it. Cortes brought with him six hundred soldiers. As he made his way to the Aztec capital, he explained the Faith to those who were receptive, baptizing tribal leaders along the way. Eventually, he arrived in the great, ancient city of Mexico. There he destroyed the last of the Aztec resistance. He understood his conquest as a holy war of liberation. "My principal motive in undertaking this war and any other one I should undertake," he explained, "is to bring the natives to the knowledge of our Holy Catholic faith." His faith was sincere. After his conquest, Cortes appealed to the Spanish crown to send Franciscan missionaries. The friars arrived, and a few years later, around 1524, Cortes established the first hospital in the New World. It was called the Hospital de la Purísma Concepción. As Cortes declared in his will, he founded this work of charity "for the graces and mercies God had bestowed on him in permitting him to discover and conquer New Spain" and also "in expiation or satisfaction for any sins he had committed."[8]

---

7 See Fray Diego Durán, *The History of the Indies of New Spain*, ch. 20, 169–72.

8 Cited in Howard Kee et al., "Christendom and Colonization," in *Christianity: A Social and Cultural History* (New York: Pearson, 1997), 529.

God seemed to confirm the new faith directly. There is a hill called Tepeyac located a few miles outside of the old city of Mexico. A new bishop had recently been installed to oversee the mission. Juan Diego was a fifty-three-year-old peasant and a recent convert. On December 9, 1531, he was on his way to hear Mass. A lady stopped him. This radiant woman, whose dress exploded with colors and the traditional symbols of his people, asked him to visit the bishop. She had a message. She wanted a new church built here, where she stood. Juan Diego reluctantly visited the bishop. The bishop sent the peasant away. "Ask for a sign," the bishop told him.

A few days later, he would receive one. On the morning of December 12, he was hurrying along a familiar path. His uncle was dying, and he was rushing to fetch a priest. The lady appeared again. This time Juan Diego tried to avoid her. She promised the uncle would be all right (the uncle in fact was healed at the moment of their meeting); again, she sent him back to the bishop. This time Juan Diego was not to appear empty handed. The woman told him to turn off the path to walk into a nearby rocky patch where he would find a cluster of roses. It was winter, but, to his surprise, he found the roses and gathered them into his arms. This, apparently, was to be the sign that would move the bishop's heart. Once Juan Diego entered the bishop's residence, he explained that the lady met him again and once more repeated her request. She wanted a church. He then unfolded his arms as the roses tumbled to the floor, to the astonishment of all. Not only were the December roses unaccountable; they were a variety particular to the bishop's native region in Spain. And beyond this, there was

Juan Diego's *tilma*. Impressed upon the front of the peasant's body was an image of the woman, Mary, who had appeared to him on the hill. Needless to say, the bishop built the church. The miraculous image survives today at Mexico's Cathedral of Our Lady of Guadalupe and attracts some ten million pilgrims each year.

Over the next twenty years, and despite the excesses of the *conquistadors*, nearly the entire population accepted the miraculous image and the Faith. In the wake of the apparitions, some twenty million Indians converted, roughly—we might note—the same number who defected from the Church during the Protestant Reformation.

~~~

But the story is yet more complicated. Not all the Spaniards were as devout as Cortes. Almost immediately after their arrival, the colonists began to enslave the Indians; almost as immediately, the clergy began to denounce those who did. The clergy wanted souls, and the colonists wanted gold; a clash was inevitable. Father Durán records how, in the early years of the conquest, some of the conquerors "even loaded ships with slaves to be carried away from New Spain." The indignant priest-chronicler describes how he saw with his own eyes Indians whose faces had been branded by Spanish masters.[9] He writes about Spanish cruelties already with the remove of some distance. The cause of this distance was not by chance; the reason was because Durán's fellow Dominicans, of a generation before, had not let such scandals pass unnoticed. One sermon stands

---

9 Durán, *The History of the Indies of New Spain*, ch. 78, 561.
~~~

out. On the Sunday before Christmas in 1511, a wealthy colonist heard a homily from one of the first missionaries, Fr. Antonio de Montesinos. As he preached to his fellow Spaniards, the Dominican spared no words. "You are all in mortal sin! You live in it and die in it! Why? Because of the cruelty and tyranny you use with these innocent people."[10] In the New World, the Indians were not serfs with grants of land, customary privileges, and opportunities for generating private wealth—as the peasants in Europe. These men were slaves, governed by masters, brutal and unchristian. One of the colonists who sat through the sermon that day was the celebrated Bartolomé de Las Casas (1474–1566).

Like St. Antony of Egypt, Las Casas heard the Lord's call and answered with resolution. He gave up his Indian slaves. He took on the habit of the Dominicans. Like his new brothers in religion, he was convinced that the Indians had souls, as did other men. They were, therefore, children of God; they were, therefore, endowed with dignity; they were, therefore, potential brothers in Christ. Las Casas helped start a movement whereby the missionaries would be sent into Indian villages to preach without interference by the Spanish troops. By 1515, he was sailing back to Spain to appeal on behalf of the Indians before the king. Las Casas later left an account of his meeting. The utter novelty and intensity of the encounter between the Spanish and the Indians can be felt in Las Casas's words in 1542, which he recorded in the third person.

> Everything that has happened since the marvelous discovery of the Americas—from the short-lived initial attempts of the

---

[10] See Kee et al., *Christianity: A Social and Cultural History*, 531.

> Spanish to settle there, right down to the present day—has been so extraordinary that the whole story remains quite incredible to anyone who has not experienced it at first hand. It seems, indeed, to overshadow all the deeds of famous men of the past, no matter how heroic, and to silence all talk of other wonders of the world. Prominent amid the aspects of this story which have caught the imagination are the massacres of innocent peoples, the atrocities committed against them and, among other horrific excesses, the ways in which towns, provinces, and whole kingdoms have been entirely cleared of their native inhabitants. Brother Bartolomé de Las Casas, or Casaus, came to the Spanish court after he entered the Order, to give our Lord, the Emperor, an eye-witness account of these enormities, not a whisper of which had at that time reached the ears of people here. He also related these same events to several people he met during his visit and they were deeply shocked by what he had to say and listened open-mouthed to his every word; they later begged him and pressed him to set down in writing a short account of some of them, and this he did.[11]

His words did not fall on deaf ears. After Las Casas returned to the new world, he was made bishop and helped draft laws promulgated in 1542 that aimed at protecting the Indians. Back in the New World, alas, he was driven from his diocese after refusing to grant absolution to obstinate colonists.

Las Casas was not alone in this struggle.[12] Other bishops followed his lead. So did a group of brilliant Spanish

---

11 Bartolomé Las Casas, *A Short Account of the Destruction of the Indies*, trans. Griffen, 3.

12 Far from it. In fact, Las Casas's zeal and exaggerations led him to be easily used by English-speaking Protestants in crafting the "Black Legend," which distorts the historical record in an effort, largely successful down to the present day, to malign all things Spanish and

Catholics, most prominent among them, Francesco di Vitoria (1492–1546), whom we met already in an earlier discussion, and Francisco Suárez (1548–1617). About the same time as Las Casas's conversion, Catholics in the Old World sought to apply the principles of moral theology to the new political realities. Ferdinand of Spain, the leading monarch of Christendom, called together a committee of theologians and lawyers to discuss the conduct of the Spanish in the New World. The result of this consultation between the Crown and the Church's intellectuals was the first piece of colonial legislation, the Law of Burgos of 1513. Vitoria had been part of this gathering. One of the fruits of this experience was that he would develop a sophisticated account of the law among nations, for which reason he, along with Hugo Grotius, is sometimes called by historians the "father of International Law."[13]

The rights of Christian peoples could be easily argued from Scripture and custom. What was less clear was the legal standing of pagan peoples before a Christian ruler. Did the Indians retain a right to their own land? Did they have to trade with the Spanish? Could they refuse to convert?

Catholic. The reality is complex, but both the Spanish crown as well as representatives of the Church sought to protect the natives against the rapaciousness of many colonists. For references, see A. Bandlier, "Bartolomé de las Casas," in *The Catholic Encyclopedia* (1908) and J. N. Hillgarth, *The Mirror of Spain, 1500–1700: The Formation of a Myth* (Ann Arbor, MI: University of Michigan Press, 2000).

13 Helpful orientation to the context and significance of Vitoria's work can be found in the introduction to *Vitoria: Political Works*, trans. and ed. Anthony Pagden and Jeremy Lawrance (Cambridge: Cambridge University Press, 2010).

From the beginning of the Spanish conquest, the government maintained that, more than the acquisition of gold, the crown desired conversion of the native peoples. Such was the aspiration. The gap between theory and practice had too often left the Indians with an ultimatum. As Las Casas had made clear, "Either they adopt the Christian religion and swear allegiance to the Crown of Castile, or they will find themselves . . . cut down or taken prisoner."[14] Part of what justified such practices was the view that the Indians satisfied Aristotle's definition of the so-called "natural slave." The wisest pagan had put it this way in his best work on politics: that person whose mind "participates in reason enough to apprehend, but not to have [independent judgments]," he opined, "is a slave by nature."[15] By this Aristotle meant natural slaves could understand commands but not issue them.

Vitoria thought Aristotle wrong. The brilliant pagan's description didn't fit the Indian's nature. The Spanish crown held over the Indians no "natural right of conquest." For their part, Vitoria argued, the Indians manifestly displayed the capacity for self-rule. Christians may go to war to liberate captives—such as those destined to human sacrifice or wanton oppression—but they have no de facto right to confiscate land. Extending the Thomistic theory of natural law, and the just war tradition, Vitoria derived one of the most important conclusions in the history of ethics, one that was to undercut every future theology of slavery. It's a truth worth contemplating today. A people may be

---

14 Las Casas, *A Short Account*, 32.

15 Aristotle, *Politics*, trans. B. Jowett, 1.5.

barbaric; they may need grace; but without doubt they possess "as true [a] dominion over their land, both public and private, as any Christians."[16] Private property is a right natural to man as man. The state that infringes the exercise of this right is a rogue power.

~~~

Still, beyond these legal gains, extraordinary as they were, more was needed. Effective reform of the missions in the New World was not achieved until control was finally wrested out of the hands of the European monarchs. The Church did this about a century later in 1622. In that year, the Vatican established an organization called the *Congregatio de Propaganda Fide,* the "Congregation for the Promotion of the Faith." The congregation, older than any modern democracy, remains active today. In evaluating the conditions of the native populations that the Spanish and Portuguese had subjugated, and the time it took for the papacy to discover an effective response to abuses, one has to consider two factors. First is the delay in communications. Travel was dangerous, sporadic, and costly. Letters took months to cross back and forth across the Atlantic. Secondly, there was the complex division of power between the Church and colonial kingdoms. Catholic political theory does not endorse the theory of the "theocratic state." The formal separation of Church and state, properly understood, is, as we noted earlier, a singular contribution of Catholic political thinking to the West. Secular rulers are to support the work of the Church. But they are never to be

16 Vitoria, *On the American Indians*, trans. Pagden and Lawrance, 250.
~~~

confused *with* the Church. And, unlike in Islam or in Old Testament Judaism, this "gap" was considered necessary if the Church was to retain her evangelical liberty of action.

After 1622, the Church seemed to regain some of her liberty. Mission territories had by this time opened up in North America, India, and Asia. The first act of the congregation was to launch a worldwide fact-finding operation. The congregation's founding secretary was Francesco Ingoli (1578–1649). What he found did not encourage. Some missionaries were involved in personally lucrative venture capital schemes—think here of the renegade mission priest in Willa Cathar's *Death Comes for the Archbishop*—they fought against one another and, above all, were failing to cultivate native ordinations. (A local council in Mexico City in 1555, for example, forbade locals from joining religious orders.)[17] Portugal and Spain resisted such interference from Rome. One example of such resistance may suffice. Among the first vicars for the new Vatican congregation was a priest named Matthew de Castro, a Brahmin convert who had studied in Rome. The pope gave him oversight of the missions in India. The Portuguese Archbishop of Goa, unfortunately, blocked these efforts and the Indian convert was forced to return to Rome, where he died in 1677.

The greatest successes in the seventeenth-century mission activity were achieved by the Jesuits. Back in Sao Paulo, the divide between the colonists and the Church had widened. Spain had by this time outlawed slavery. The Portuguese, however, were not so constrained. Slave traders regularly attacked Spanish-Indian settlements. In 1629, for

---

17 See Kee et al., *Christianity: A Social and Cultural History*, 533.

instance, these man-hunters captured some fifteen thousand Indians to sell to the Portuguese markets.

While the Spanish government did not condone the actions, neither did they significantly interfere, as the British eventually would some two centuries later. But where the princes lay dormant, the Jesuits launched their own offensive. In response to the trade, they gathered thousands of the native villagers and conducted them some four thousand miles along a mass evacuation. The next year, in 1642, the Jesuits established new villages out of the reach of the slave-hunters.[18] A popular movie from the 1980s, *The Mission*, offers an evocative depiction of these model villages. The Guarani Indians, as they came to be called, lived a semi-monastic, joy-filled life, ordered around the Christian year of fasts and feasts; they built magnificent churches and created a unique musical repertoire that blended Baroque with their own native sounds.

In Canada, the Jesuits attempted a similar experiment in communal living with the Huron Indians. Prior to his martyrdom, St. Jean de Brébeuf (1593–1649) and his companions had cataloged their customs and religious beliefs and made a dictionary of the Huron tongue. Their goal was to teach the Hurons not only the Faith but the skills of farming that would allow them to rise above a nomadic and impoverished existence. The Jesuits came on a mission of mercy. The earliest, most complete account of the customs of the native peoples of North America is contained in the histories and letters of these noble souls. Their letters show forth both the ignorance and the beauty of these unlettered

---

18 Ibid., 540, and "Guarní Indians" in *The Catholic Encyclopedia* (1910).

peoples. We see also these highly educated Frenchmen struggling to adapt themselves and their manners to a people who have no patience for the refined culture of Europeans. The harsh conditions of the Canadian winter may have left the Indians with little time or inclination to study; but they were astute readers of souls. Paul le Jeune, one of the early martyrs, explained to the eager reading public in France in a letter of 1635 just prior to his death: "Our theology is difficult for them to understand, but they comprehend perfectly our humility and friendliness," as he noted, "and through these they are won."[19]

Their experiments in founding Christian villages partially succeeded. The men won converts. Yet the missionaries and scores of Indians lost their lives. The Hurons not only caught European diseases; they also lost their homes to the fierce Iroquois who in 1635 killed Paul le Jean and wiped out most of the Huron villages. Those who survived fled to Montreal or melted into other Indian communities.

~~~

Was the Church's transformation of the New World for the good? Some have thought not. And it is reasonable to ask whether the Church always worked enough to protect the indigenous peoples that it served. Surely, at many points, the Church could have done better. But no entity in the history of the world, I think, would have done more. Through her preaching, her teaching, and her sacraments,

---

19 From a 1635 Letter of Paul le Jeune, S. J., in *Jesuit Missionaries to North America: Spiritual Writings and Biographical Sketches*, trans. and ed. Francois Roustang (San Francisco, CA: Ignatius Press, 2006), 102.
~~~

the Church's missionaries, often against the wishes of the European powers, though sometimes with their generous support, brought to native peoples the seeds of moral rejuvenation, the tools of technology, and above all, the message of salvation.

"The Church has never preached social revolution," declared Pope Pius XII in 1951 during a radio address to Spanish workers. Nevertheless, the news that Christ had opened up heaven was bound to transform how men conducted themselves on earth. This is true of political structures in general and of slavery in particular. In popular histories, the Church is often presented as an oppressor of women, of slaves, and, since colonial times, as a conspirator with kings against the poor. The Church indeed has never offered a gospel merely of social revolution. What it delivered was a message far more liberating. Henceforth, man, woman, slave, free, Jew, and Gentile are "one in Christ." Against the Marxist interpretation of history as the story of class struggle, the pope continued in his message to the Spanish workers: "Always and everywhere . . . she has worked hard to have more concern shown for the human being than for economic and technical advantages, and to get as many as possible, on their part, to do all they can to live a Christian life and one worthy of a human being."[20]

That simple message of reconciliation did more for the oppressed throughout history than has any war of liberation. Concepts such as "human rights" and "the dignity of the person" and the individual's "conscience" have entered

---

[20] The text of Pius's speech is available at http://www.stthomas.edu/media/catholicstudies/center/johnaryaninstitute/publications/publicationpdfs/piusxiipdf/Pius_Section_II_51-53.pdf.

into contemporary secular discourse, but they arose first at the insistence of the Catholic Church: Christ had won for broken humanity a new brotherhood and the liberty to be called sons of God.

Over the next two centuries, Europe would fight wars at home over the definition of that liberty.

10

REVOLUTIONARIES: THE UNEXPECTED GIFT OF THÉRÈSE

"I wanted to find an elevator which would raise me to Jesus."

St. Thérèse of Lisieux

MODERNITY is not one "thing." Indeed, it does not follow a single script. It is, rather, a sequence of isolated plots whose master ideas continue to be drawn from the old Christian story, but without the confidence to name just who are its lead characters or how the drama will end. Is man a clever angel or a dull ape? Is freedom an illusion or the foundation of rights? Should politics aim for an international order or protect the interests of race, color, or sex? During the eighteenth and nineteenth centuries, in the era of revolutionary wars and politics, thinkers in the West began, for the first time since Constantine, to frame questions in terms no longer drawn consistently from Scripture and the Catholic intellectual tradition. Concepts like universal rights, human dignity, social justice, and progress enter the vernacular of the West in this era. These are each terms that find their origins in Christian tradition. And yet they will be used for alien purposes. Instead of ordering politics and family life under the light of eternity, where the goods of this world are seen to find their ultimate fulfillment in the next, the aspirations of modern Western people began to turn from the City of God to the City of Man.

If it were possible to locate the site of the quarrel between the old world—the West as it had been shaped by centuries of Christian customs and belief—and the emerging new world of secular modernity, we might find it in the debate over two accounts of *hope*. Where Christians find strength to do good in this world in the hope of God's final reckoning and reward for our efforts, leading secular thinkers sought to turn our aspirations for the future kingdom to the present world. The enduring gift of the Church to the West in these centuries is her witness of perseverance under persecution and her proclamation of the true meaning of hope, a proclamation that found eloquent expression in the life of a little girl from the French town of Lisiuex.

~~~

On July 14, 1789, revolutionaries stormed the Bastille, a political prison in Paris that symbolized the royal power. Every prisoner was freed. All seven of them. Hardly an auspicious beginning to the end of the ancient regime. But the power of the mob had been set loose, and the Catholic Church was now to enter the most ferocious period of persecution yet experienced in her long history.

The French revolutionaries were led by intelligent, cynical men. Historians have subsequently dubbed the seventeenth and eighteenth centuries the Age of Reason; in a less compressed form, this means the age was marked by a revival of Stoic philosophy, empirical science, republican
~~~

government, and a rebellion against revealed religion. The architects of the European Enlightenment disagreed on many matters. What united its leading figures—such as John Locke (1632–1704), Jean-Jacques Rousseau (1712–78), and Voltaire (1694–1778)—was disdain for the Catholic Church. For all John Locke's praise of religious toleration, he was clear that Catholics, along with atheists, could never be regarded as loyal citizens of Britain; atheists, because fear of hell couldn't hold them to their promises, and Catholics, because their first allegiance was to a foreign sovereign, the pope.[1] Rousseau, for his part, tried to found his own religion. He denied original sin, preached a natural piety, and thought men should be "forced to be free" by the power of the sword.[2] This sentiment would be translated into policy over the coming years.

Of all the dozens of *philosophes* and intellectual architects of the French Revolution, however, Voltaire is most emblematic. The Church's relentless critic—to which he referred at times simply as *l'enfâme*, "the infamy"—he was a brilliant pamphleteer, writing some forty thousand letters filled with the righteous indignation of an Elijah. He considered Christianity vile. He believed God's will absolutely inscrutable.[3] He thought that priests incited intolerance and

---

1 Locke, *Letter on Toleration*, ed. Tully, 50.

2 Rousseau, *Social Contract and Discourses*, 1.7.

3 Where Protestants and Catholics tried to read "purposes" off of such events as the earthquake that devastated Lisbon 1 November 1755, Voltaire scoffed. He thinks divine purposes can never be read off of events. He ends one entry in his *Portable Philosophical Dictionary* (1764), for instance, with the following: "Let us place at the end of almost all the chapters on metaphysics the two letters the Roman judges employed when they did not understand a lawsuit: *N.L., non*

that their doctrines encouraged superstition. And for all that, he seems to have taken the goodness of the Church for granted. At least the Church helped the poor. He could, for instance, recount with fondness his early education at the hands of her ministers. "What did I see during the seven years that I was with the Jesuits?" he once asked. "The most industrious, frugal, regulated life; all their hours divided between the care they took of us and the exercises of their austere profession."[4]

Voltaire was France's philosophical millionaire. On his estate he kept thirty servants, and, loving to keep company with princes, his private behavior was at times extravagantly decadent; neither convention nor disparity in age could keep him away from a romantic involvement with a lady who happened to be nearly two decades his junior, and his niece.[5] Even so, for all his spiteful vitriol against religion, he could be personally generous. He wished the common man to remain constrained by the old disciplines. At times he even kept up appearances: he encouraged his workers to send their children to catechism class; he constructed a chapel on his estates, was active in a Catholic lay order, read sermons during dinner, and on occasion attended Mass.[6]

One of the abiding ironies of the European Enlightenment is how decidedly parochial the event was. On the

---

liquet; this isn't clear." In Voltaire, *Candide and Related Texts*, trans. David Wootton (Indianapolis, IN: Hackett, 2000), 142.

4 Durant, *Age of Voltaire*, 4.

5 See Ian Davidson *Voltaire: A Life* (New York: Pegasus Books, 2010), 206.

6 See Crocker, *Triumph*, 334.

level of theory, the conclusions of "universal reason" were discovered by men raised by the Church, or at least who fed off her remains. Once the ideas of the revolutionaries began to be put into effect, it was unclear what would be left for the philosophers to consume. Voltaire never lived to see the success of his own campaigns; he wrote his incendiary letters in relative peace. It would be left to others to live through the fire.

By 1793, the blaze raged. King Louis XVI had been executed. In a single day in Paris, three hundred priests were martyred. Those clerics who wished to keep their necks had been forced to sign up to the *Civil Constitution of the Clergy*, a bill passed on 12 July 1790; this law wrested control of the priests out of the hands of Rome and reduced the Church to a branch of civil government. Clergy who refused either fled, were murdered, or ministered in forests. At Notre Dame Cathedral, revolutionaries dressed up a lewd woman as the "goddess of reason" in a parody of the Mass. In the area of the Vendée, where Catholics loyal to the crown raised arms against the atheists and deists, thousands of civilians were butchered by Revolutionary troops. By these means did the glorious slogans of the philosophers—liberty, equality, and fraternity—open onto France and across all of Europe the churning waters of bloodshed, war, and persecution.[7]

At no time have Christians suffered more violent and systematic persecutions than during the French Revolution

---

[7] For arresting accounts of the Catholic peasant uprising, see Michael Davies, *For Altar and Throne: The Rising in the Vendee* (St. Paul, MN: Remnant Press, 1997) and Anthony Trollope, *La Vendée: An Historical Romance* (1850).

and the era of its afterglow. Prior to the Revolution, persecution had for the most part been the product of passion; after the Revolution, persecution had become a matter of policy. Over roughly the first decade of the nineteenth century, for instance, the pope would be a prisoner to French troops twice—his second imprisonment at the hands of Napoleon in 1809. After the French general seized Pius VII, he dragged the pontiff north across the mountains to Grenoble and to Savona, where he kindly offered Pius an annual stipend in exchange for papal territories. The pope baulked. Infuriated, Napoleon confiscated his prisoner's books, paper, even his papal ring. Pius VII would only be released five years later, on 10 March 1814, once Napoleon saw that his war against Britain, Russia, Prussia, and Austria would fail.

The French experience provided a template for other nations. There would be civil wars and persecutions against Catholics in nineteenth-century Germany under Bismarck, through the 1920s and 1930s in Mexico, during the Communist attempt to liquidate Eastern Orthodoxy and Catholicism, during Spain's civil war, and yet again under Hitler and Mao in mid-century. In a century filled to the brim with government-sponsored killing, it is difficult to weigh which of the revolutions inflicted greater suffering. Still, arguably the ugliest child of the revolutionary era, the one with the most lasting cultural effects, was born in London in the British Library. That's where Karl Marx penned his *Communist Manifesto*.

~~~

What happens when brothers lose their father? What becomes of the *Imago Dei* when the original is no more? What happens to justice and solidarity when men abandon the God of the Bible? Concrete proposals to these questions were forthcoming. When Marx published his work in 1848, conditions for the working classes were bleak. Destruction of the old guilds had isolated workers; factories drained the countryside of peasants and elevated industrialists to the status of monarchs. Marx identified accurately both the plight of the new poor and the effect of the new commerce. As capitalism advanced, he saw that local customs, domestic habits, even national characteristics all tended to dissolve in the acid of so-called economic necessity. Marx saw correctly how soon capitalism would make Cairo and Tokyo and New York look very much like Birmingham. Devotion to the old gods was being displaced by devotion, as he remarked, to "cheap prices."[8]

If the philosopher's diagnosis was sound, his starting point was less sure. Marxism is based on the principle of materialism, the view that everything that can be known or thought can be observed through the senses. Such a view fits well only if you hold your eye to a narrow lens. Anything in man that suggests a spiritual nature must be explained away. It also led Marx to draw a series of destructive conclusions. With no conception of the spiritual, thought, too, must be reduced to material forces—that is to say, to brute power. As Marx saw, when reason no

---

8 Marx, *Communist Manifesto*, trans. Jones, 224.
~~~

longer mediates between men, conflict becomes inevitable. Revolution becomes the chief instrument of peace.

Like every other of the leading modern philosophers, Marx sought a unitary principle that could collect experience under a single umbrella. Since René Descartes's *cogito ergo sum*, "I think therefore I am," European intellectuals found themselves locked in a game of hide and seek. Tradition they abjured. Christianity they had lost. What they sought in desperation was to find candidates for their replacement. In the new Age of Enlightenment, the redemption of human nature required that the identities of men and women be reconstructed from ground zero. Indeed, the revolutionaries in France made the point explicit when they abolished the "old" calendar. Instead of measuring time from the birth of Jesus Christ, they set their clocks back to the razing of the Bastille, the freeing of those seven men, or alternatively to the founding of the Republic in 1792. Gone was the seven-day week. Found was a new decade by which citizens were to regulate their lives: the ten-day workweek.

If not for their wisdom, at least we may credit the revolutionaries for their ambition. With only their own wits to guide, what the architects of the Enlightenment searched to find were answers to the abiding riddles of human existence. How do we know? How shall we live? What orders history? In the reading room of the British Library, Karl Marx thought he had finally uncovered the key.

History, Marx averred, is nothing other than the record of the progress of class struggle. Power is at the root of all interactions. Inequalities create pressure points in the flow of this ceaseless movement of peoples. Conflict, he thought, is the cosmic constant that levels artificial barriers, the inexorable tide that corrodes the sand castles of custom and religion and the thousand loves that endear men and women to their neighborhoods and farms. This insight shot across his vision like a comet from heaven. Like Luther's *sola fide*, Marx thought every facet of human life could be interpreted through this master lens. As the opening line of his *Communist Manifesto* declares, "The history of all hitherto existing society is the history of class struggles."[9] The idea appealed especially to men with empty heads and open pockets; that is, men without metaphysics or decent work. The disciples of Marx followed a scorched-earth policy. The gulags, the KGB priest-hunts, the bullet in the chest of John Paul II, the some 100 million dead, all of these, as well as the Church's heroic opposition, are well known, or at least well documented. As one scholar of Marxism put it, Communist regimes "turned mass crime into a full-blown system of government."[10] What is perhaps less appreciated is the longer-term devastation that Marxism unleashed upon the family. On this front, the hammer of Marx has only begun to fall.

We do well not to forget that, for Marxists, even before the destruction of the nation, the first enemy of equality is the family. Women get pregnant. Men can work longer hours. Thus the union of man and woman is a contract

---

9 Marx, *Communist Manifesto*, 219.

10 This observation made by Stephen Courtois, editor of *The Black Book of Communism: Crimes, Terror, Repression* (Cambridge, MA: Harvard University Press, 1999), 2. On the Catholic Church's role in dismantling Communism, see George Weigel, *Witness to Hope: The Biography of Pope John Paul II* (New York: Harper Collins, 1999).

between economic un-equals. This he thought unfair. Marriage presents another, more fundamental problem for Marxists. Simply, marriage begets a polity that rivals the regime. After World War Two, America and her allies made clear their intention to combat the spread of Communism. At this point, leading Marxist intellectuals began to change tactics by returning to one of Marx's earlier insights about the family. It is the economic inequality between men and women that led Marx to call family the first instance of slavery, and it was the political stalemate of the Cold War that led Marxists to shift the efforts of the revolution to a new theatre of conflict: culture and law. The conquest over the nuclear, heterosexual family that Marx himself could not achieve by a direct assault was in later years carried forward by his disciples in the West with arguably greater success.

The irony should not be lost. That the same liberal democracies that sacrificed their blood and treasure to preserve liberty against Communist bombs and bullets should have capitulated so quickly before Communist ideas is surely one of the unexpected reversals of twentieth-century politics. State childcare, state schools, state abortions, and state economies are all practices first systematically put into practice by our enemies in the name of universal equality. Now that the United States has joined the rest of NATO in embracing homosexual unions, it would seem that the back of the family has finally been broken, that one of the last natural pockets of resistance to what Hilaire Belloc once called the "servile state" has been undermined.

~~~

If the nineteenth century saw the birth of godless revolutions, it also saw the rebirth of an invigorated Church. Not only did the Church survive the relentless confiscations and deportations of the century of "progress"; she emerged from them with an inexplicable strength. It is one of the paradoxes of faith that in the proportion that men hope in power, God raises up the weak and that in the proportion that men grow proud in the use of their reason, God exalts the humble. No other explanation can account for the gift of the girl from Lisieux.

Perhaps it was a way of answering the proud sneers of Voltaire or the hardened atheism of Marx. Perhaps it was a way of giving hope to the suffering. Where men might have looked for a new St. Thomas, or hoped for another Benedict or Dominic or Ignatius, God sent us a little girl from an insignificant place. God sent us Thérèse. The nineteenth century had its share of spiritual giants. In Italy, John Bosco rescued boys from prison and the streets; in America, St. Francis Cabrini taught the children of Italian immigrants; in England, John Henry Newman preached to professors. Yet with all due devotion, none of these has left an imprint in the soil of the Catholic imagination as have the light footprints of the girl of the Little Way.

St. Thérèse was born in 1873 to a middle-class family in a modest French village of Alençon, population 13,600. She was the youngest of nine children. When her mother died of breast cancer, Thérèse's older sister, Pauline, cared for Thérèse as though she had become her adopted daughter. Thérèse followed her older sisters into the nearby
~~~

Carmelite monastery. Like any other religious sister, she too struggled to fulfill her vows. She hardly traveled. She found some sisters hard to bear. Under obedience, she wrote an account of her life. She suffered from tuberculosis and was dead at twenty-four. In outline this describes the life of an obscure French girl, with the difference that this girl's death marked merely the beginning of her effect.

Almost immediately after Thérèse's passing from this life, word of miracles began to circulate back to the cloister. She had sought during her few years at Carmel to live what she called "the little way," a path to holiness through ordinary means. She sought, as she said, "a means of going to heaven by a little way, a way that is very straight, very short, and totally new." She explained her method in the following terms:

> We are living now in an age of inventions, and we no longer have to take the trouble of climbing stairs, for, in the homes of the rich, an elevator has replaced these very successfully. I wanted to find an elevator which would raise me to Jesus, for I am too small to climb the rough stairway of perfection. I searched, then, in the Scripture for some sign of this elevator, the object of my desires, and I read these words coming from the mouth of Eternal Wisdom: "Whoever is a LITTLE ONE, let him come to me." And so I succeeded.[11]

During Thérèse's last years, her little way led to what might have seemed a dead end. She fell ill. Added to that, she experienced what St. John of the Cross described as the "dark night" of the soul. It was as though the sunshine of God's face hid itself from his little flower. God pulled back.

---

11 St. Thérèse, *Story of a Soul: The Autobiography of St. Thérèse of Lisieux*, trans. Clarke, 3rd ed., 207.

In her autobiography, Thérèse is articulate about the spiritual disorientation into which she now descended. A fog engulfed her. Heaven looked unreal. Taunting voices rang in her ears, words uttered by the spirit of the times: "You are dreaming about the light, about a fatherland embalmed in the sweetest perfumes. . . . Advance, advance; rejoice in death which will give you not what you hope for but a night still more profound, the night of nothingness."[12]

To Karl Marx, religion was an opiate; to Sigmund Freud, God was a projection of the father. The twentieth century was plagued by such suggestions. It's as though Thérèse anticipated and experienced in herself all the tortured doubt, all the twisted anguish that the poison of public atheism would release into the atmosphere we moderns breathe.

Unlike the world-weary masters of the age, however, Thérèse's will never broke. She was too strong for weak doubt. As she waded through the darkness, she learned to lean upon the smooth-handled staff of the saints: she mastered perseverance; she continued to work, to pray, and to hope. To her superior, she admitted, "While I do not have *the joy of faith*, I am trying to carry out its works at least." The divine lover is coy. He tests our desire. "I believe that I have made more acts of faith in this past year than all through my whole life."[13] The little flower did not fade. As death approached, she promised that she would spend her eternity doing good on the earth, and she kept her word. Within weeks of her passing, the monastery was unable to keep up with the correspondence. Dozens and

---

12 Ibid., 213.

13 Ibid.

then hundreds of letters per week rolled into the cloister. An army of sister-clerks was appointed to sort through the mail. A mere twenty-eight years later, Pope Pius XI canonized Thérèse, whom Pope John Paul II would later declare a Doctor of the Church.

We may ask, "Why did God send Thérèse?" The Church, to be sure, has never been lacking in brilliant minds and devoted servants; yet a different sort of remedy was needed. The unaffected simplicity of Thérèse seemed the medicine suited to the sickness of that century and the next. In a sermon delivered in London, the twentieth-century English convert Fr. Ronald Knox reflected on the particular gift of St. Thérèse for the West:

> It was, and is, an over-educated age that needs to sit at the feet of an under-educated saint. We must go to her for lessons in simplicity, because our own brains are tired out and distracted by the multiplicity of the world in which we live; its clashing interests, its jarring battle-cries, its irreconcilable philosophies. We have got to learn that the way to God for this or that soul is not through comparing and contrasting all these rival claims upon our intellectual adhesion, making a synthesis of them and reducing them to theology. The way to God lies in turning our backs on these images, shutting our ears to these interruptions, and adhering to him by a simple, personal approach, by cultivating a sense of the intimacy by which he makes himself immediately present to the Christian soul. We thought, perhaps, that in such an age of intellectual bewilderment he would send us a second St. Thomas, to solve our difficulties for us. He sent us, instead, Soeur Thérèse, to teach us they were not the point.[14]

---

14 Ronald Knox, "On Christian Education" homily delivered at an event in aid of London's Oratory School, in *Renewing the Mind: A Reader in the Philosophy of Catholic Education*, ed. Topping (Washington, D.C.: Catholic University of America Press, 2015), 267–68.

Along similar lines, during her beatification, Pope Benedict XV declared, "In spiritual childhood is the secret of sanctity for all the faithful of the Catholic world." And again, years later, when a journalist asked the next (future) Pope Benedict why the little flower should have been named "Doctor" of the Church, a title usually reserved for an elite company of theologians, Cardinal Ratzinger replied that Thérèse shows us another side of the Church's teaching ministry.

> It is important, in our scientific society, to have the message of a simple and deep experience of God, and a teaching about the simplicity of being a saint: in this time, with all its extremely action-oriented approach, [Thérèse's life teaches] that to be a saint is not necessarily a matter of great actions, but [of] letting the Lord work in us.[15]

In the midst of an era of upheavals, and of destructive politics in the name of secular "progress," Catholicism offered to the West not only an argument but a living image of hope founded not on politics and technology but on love. Through her saints, and in an extraordinary way, through the life of St. Thérèse, God imparted to the Church a new tenderness and a new hope; that gift would be needed by the faithful and by the popes that would lead them into the twentieth and twenty-first centuries.

---

15 Interview with George Weigel, 20 September 1997, in *God's Choice: Pope Benedict XVI and the Future of the Catholic Church* (New York: HarperCollins Publisher, 2005), 285.

11

POPES: THE GIFT OF A NEW EVANGELIZATION

"Do not be satisfied with mediocrity. Put out into the deep."
St. Pope John Paul II

THE century and more after Thérèse has been, for the Church, a time of spiritual giants and crushing disasters, an era of abundant prosperity and of ferocious opposition. In few periods has the Church militant benefited from such a succession of brilliant popes; certainly at no time, at least since the Reformation, has she suffered from more defections and public dissent from her ministers. The defining event of the past one hundred years for the Church has been the Second Vatican Council (1962–65). In marking the direction these popes have taken the Church, and the more recent gifts imparted, we'll follow their interventions before, during, and after the council and see how they've prepared the Church of the twenty-first century for a new era of evangelism.

~~~

When Pope Pius IX died in 1878, not long after Garibaldi's men had united Italy and forced the cardinals to flee Rome in the midst of the First Vatican Council (1870), the
~~~

pontiff's body was carried to San Lorenzo. Along the way, a Roman mob attacked the procession and attempted to toss the coffin into the Tiber. The priests eventually beat back the crowd. But the incident highlights the intense animosity that the revolutionary spirit had incited against the papacy by the end of the nineteenth century. Pius IX's successor was Cardinal Pecci. Pope Leo XIII (1878–1903) was a man of sharp intellect and granite will. The two greatest contributions of his papacy, from which the Church continues to benefit, emanated from his two most memorable encyclicals: *Aeterni Patris* (1878), on education, and *Rerum Novarum* (1891), on work.

Catholic intellectual life in the nineteenth century did not sparkle. In part, this was a natural consequence of the disruptions of her academies. In France, for example, Napoleon had closed all Catholic universities within his territory, while in Bismarck's Germany, half the bishops were either in exile or in prison due to their resistance to his *Kulturfampf*, or "cultural struggle," a conflict that centered largely around control of the schools. Famously, after Cardinal Newman left Oxford and first came into contact with theologians in Rome, he was dismayed at their formulaic approach to theology. Phrases had come to substitute for thought. As for Protestants, 1878 was the springtime for so-called "higher" biblical criticism. Belief in miracles, the inspiration of Scripture, and even the divinity of Christ all fell under suspicion as the foundation for Protestant belief, the Bible, was tried and found wanting by the new science of historical exegesis. Darwin disproved Adam. Sigmund Freud unveiled the "id." J. S. Mill rendered license a liberty, and Adam Smith's economics reduced providence to an "invisible hand." Science was advancing, but the West's noble tradition of philosophy was, by the measure of orthodoxy at least, spiraling toward the black hole of skepticism. Pope Leo sought to regain the initiative. He understood well that eventually politics follows culture and that culture depends upon the cultivation of the mind. His call was for a return to St. Thomas.

Leo's encyclical *Aeterni Patris* (*On the Restoration of Christian Philosophy*) is not so much a call to reflection as a summons to a coordinated effort. He reminds his readers of philosophy's indispensable aid to religion: it can "smooth and fortify" the mind's path toward faith; it binds together doctrines so that the whole of theology "may join together"; as for answering skeptical objections, rightly trained reason can even "religiously" defend truths known only by faith.[1] He then turns to history. The Church's tradition of scholarship is vast; starting with the era of the Apologists, and then the early Fathers, Leo runs his readers swiftly along the peaks of nearly twenty centuries of Christian philosophy, from Augustine and Basil to Anselm and Damascene to the high Scholastics. Among them all, he recommends St. Thomas.

The merit Leo sees in Thomas Aquinas is twofold. Thomas offers firm starting principles and judiciously divides the methods of the sciences. Thomas starts from the principle of romantic realism. He is romantic insofar as he knows reason is fitted to know the highest things and realistic inasmuch as he starts from consideration of the lowest things. For St. Thomas, the good philosopher walks with

---

1 Leo XIII, *Aeterni Patris* (1879), 6–7.

his head up and with his feet planted firmly upon the earth. With Aristotle, and the empiricists, Thomas accepts that knowledge begins with the senses; like Plato and the idealists, he understands that it could never be satisfied with resting there. Knowledge of God, freedom, and morality all find their surest foundations, Leo suggests, in the principles of Thomas. Proving God is no small thing. But with a prophet's intuition, Leo recognized that Thomas's greatest contribution to modern thought would likely lie elsewhere: in reforming our thinking about science.[2]

It is here, in our thinking about method, that Thomas will yield decisive advantages. St. Thomas was a master organizer. He knew how to give each science its proper due. He understood, in particular, how to keep reason from being confused with or, better, simply absorbed by faith and how to help each authority enrich the other. It may not at first be clear why a division among varying approaches to truth is important. A little reflection, however, makes clear the kinds of needless civil wars of the mind that Leo hoped to avert—as in the past when some theologians attempted to count the years from the creation of the world, or when neuroscientists today try to reduce mind to matter. Judging from John Paul II's speech before the Pontifical Academy of Sciences, which closed a decade-long inquiry into the Church's unfortunate condemnation of Galileo in the seventeenth century, it would appear that the Catholic Church has, after centuries of further reflection, well absorbed the sort of distinctions Thomas had proposed already in the thirteenth century. What is less clear is whether those who

---

2 Ibid., 29.

claim to speak on behalf of the hard sciences have undergone an analogous period of soul-searching.

Catholic theologians have for many generations appreciated the rightful autonomy of the hard sciences. At times natural scientists don't seem inclined to reciprocate the courtesy. Not uncommonly, they will wander outside of their own proper terrain. Without the benefit of philosophy or theology, they not infrequently get lost; when their microscope doesn't discover God or the soul, some falsely presume these are nowhere to be found. Listen, for example, to the breezy confidence with which New York University's professor of neuroscience Dr. Rodolfo Llinas can dismiss free will, human consciousness, and the basis for ethics: "Some people believe we are something beyond neurons, but of course we are not. We are just the sum total of the activity of neurons. We assume that we have free will and that we make decisions, but we don't. Neurons do. We decide that this sum total driving us is a decision we have made for ourselves. But it is not."[3]

This description nicely echoes the popular biologist Richard Dawkins's more poetic declaration that life "is just bytes and bytes and bytes of digital information."[4] How, precisely, could this scientist's method yield such conclusions? Consider: if consciousness truly was nothing more than the product of electrical pulses, or if thought were nothing greater than the outcome of random processes, why should we trust it? Random inputs, rational outputs? We

---

3 "The Electric Brain," *Nova*, PBS, October 23, 2001, http://www.pbs.org/wgbh/nova/body/electric-brain.html.

4 Richard Dawkins, *A River out of Eden: A Darwinian View of Life* (New York: Basic Books, 2008), 19.

would never entrust our brakes to a mechanic who worked from such a principle. Why should we entrust our brains to such a doctor? But of course, the professor's calculated activities are better than his theory. One has to think only of the dozens of rational decisions that feed into a scientific experiment to begin to sense the inherent contradictions that flow from dismissing reason by an act of reason. In every scientific study, questions must be stated, instruments must be tested, observations must be recorded, and inferences must be drawn. Alas, in this case, the scientist's conclusion undermines his method. That's the first problem with such weak thinking. Materialists use reason to dismiss thought.

The second problem with a philosophically rootless science is that it substitutes myth for argument. Instead of man being the actor, some other less understood entity is called in to stand in his place. The brain, neurons, or even evolution itself becomes the magical fairy that pulls strings behind the curtain. Man is the machine; mystical forces become the real source of life. Consider how Dr. Llinas answers an objection. Aware that the elimination of free will is a somewhat awkward position to hold, in his defense, the professor appeals to Darwin: "The brain," he explains, "has been beautifully assembled by evolution." Pause there. Assembled by whom? By what mind? Presumably the scientist intended his statement to be poetic. What it is not is philosophically rigorous. Note the equivocation. When materialists speak of purposes, design, beauty, or intention as this professor does, they appeal to just the sort of things that materialism was supposed to explain away: a directing mind. They tell us all rabbits are dead, and then pull one out of their hat.

But we need not be so mystical. Evolution, as a description of emergent complexity, poses no threat either to science or to religion. It's only when evolution becomes a substitute for God that the theory poses a problem. Then it's bad science—or no science at all—and it's bad religion. Getting rid of God by appealing to vast ages is like trying to get rid of a tennis ball by throwing it against a brick wall: all the phenomena you wanted to explain away—an intelligent soul, an intelligible universe, and an intellectual Maker—keep bouncing back at you. In short, science severed from philosophy ends up suppressing obvious observations. On the soul, we are asked to deny that mind is essentially different from matter; on the universe, we are asked to believe *something* can come from nothing; on God, well, what we can't see, we're told, can't be proved. But God never stops raising his hand, no matter how often we ignore him. Humankind's near universal experience of love, beauty, order, and prayer won't let us suppress recurring facts, no matter what the scientist's theory says is allowed. So, circumventing philosophy, leaving first principles unexamined, and dismissing overwhelming testimonial evidence, too many of our scientists are reduced to parading theories of the meaning of life held together by arguments no stiffer than chewing gum. The superstitious we will always have with us. No superstition is more common today than the superstition that science has resolved all the questions of philosophy and religion.

~~~

It is possible that materialism would have become the default position anyway. Leo's aspiration one hundred and
~~~

forty years ago was that an early exposure to St. Thomas might confront such neuroscientists and others with the potential weaknesses inherent in their own thought. His hope was that distinctions, such as between material and formal causes, or that arguments, such as St. Thomas's Five Ways of coming to know God's existence, or that reasonable divisions between methods, such as in Thomas's partitioning between mathematical, empirical, moral, and theological sciences, might offer thoughtful seekers a rationally compelling alternative. And for many scientists, Leo's call did find a ready welcome. John Paul II's magisterial 1998 encyclical *Fides et Ratio* (*On Faith and Reason*) offered an updated reaffirmation of Leo's call: don't abandon reason! Let us hope many more in the coming century will heed these invitations and the warnings contained within them. If there is a cosmos, an ordered whole, then, with Leo, man has hope that he may find a creator; if a chaos, then, with New York University's Professor Llinas, we are trapped inside a metal cage of necessary causes.

What makes Leo's work remarkable was the effect it exerted upon the Church until the Second Vatican Council. Leo ends his letter with an appeal, a caution, and a fatherly command directed specifically toward the Catholic world. His appeal was to bishops and Catholic educators: "We exhort you . . . to restore the golden wisdom of St. Thomas," and even more, "to spread it far and wide for the defense and beauty of the Catholic faith, for the good of society, and for the advantage of all sciences." Leo wished to see a renewal of institutions. His call was followed by a word of caution. It is not the slavish imitation of St. Thomas or any other philosopher that Leo recommends. Indeed, nothing of the past that "ill agrees with the discoveries of a later age" should be repeated. Leo did not wish scholars merely to become Thomists. Rather, it was the *spirit* of St. Thomas that Leo impressed upon students of the coming Catholic revival. Lastly, a fatherly command. Renewal would require vigilant oversight over faculty appointments: "Let carefully selected teachers endeavor to implant the doctrine of Thomas Aquinas in the minds of students, and set forth clearly his solidity and excellence over others."[5] Over the next two generations, Leo's efforts would bear a worthy harvest.

In 1889 *Aeterni Patris* breathed new oxygen into the system of Catholic colleges and schools throughout the world. The most favorable conditions were found in the United States. The first Catholic school in the United States was established in 1606 by Franciscans in Florida. Between the late nineteenth century and the end of the Second World War, the number of Catholic schools in the United States ballooned. In 1900 some ten million Catholics sustained 3,500 Catholic schools; by the mid-1960s, Catholic schools enrolled 5.5 million students (today Catholic schools educate under 2 million students). If the wealth of the republic, along with the surge of Irish immigration, provided the mast and poles, it was Leo's encyclical that blew a warm breeze into these sails. Elsewhere across the continent, new Catholic universities would be established and new institutes devoted to Thomas Aquinas would flourish, notably at the Pontifical Institute of Medieval Studies in Toronto and at Notre Dame.[6] Prior to the Second Vatican Council,

5 Leo XIII, *Aeterni Patris*, 31.

6 For statistics on Catholic education, see Topping, *The Case for Catholic Education* (Kettering, OH: Angelico Press, 2015), especially chapter 2.

even those professors dissatisfied with Thomism at Catholic universities usually did not object to Thomas himself but only to one or other line of his interpreters.

Leo's other major contribution was to politics. His 1891 encyclical *Rerum Novarum* (*Rights and Duties of Capital and Labor*) is always cited as the starting point of the tradition of Catholic social teaching—not to be confused with some Catholics' view of social teaching. And this is true enough, in so far as it goes. But beginning in this way with Leo can sometimes impart false impressions. It has led some to suppose that there is a year one for the tradition; it has led others to suppose that social teaching can detach itself from the rest of Catholic doctrine. The Catholic Church has always been interested in social justice and the common good. It was, after all, the Catholic Church that invented most of the social institutions that we in the West today (and everywhere else) cherish. Hospitals, universities, and even life insurance agencies all had their origins in Catholic social concern (these arose in the ninth, thirteenth, and nineteenth centuries respectively). The Church has since Pentecost been devoted to public acts of mercy even if it has not always felt the need to theorize about these acts in relation to contemporary social and economic structures. Leo theorized.

~~~

Leo's thought proved fruitful. Later popes repeatedly returned to this text in their efforts to develop such concepts as subsidiarity, solidarity, the culture of life, and the
~~~

dignity of the family.[7] John Paul II's distinctive contribution to the Leonine tradition came in 1991 just after the fall of communism in the form of his third encyclical, *Centesimus Annus* (*Hundredth Year*). In this brilliant though controversial work, he posited that culture was the real engine of history, including economic history; he proposed, further, that the free economy, properly understood as the form of exchange which honored and encouraged human ingenuity and responsibility, was the one most closely aligned with the dignity of the person.

The Church's social teaching would develop in other directions too. In the midst of this diversity, sometimes Catholics and non-Catholics have wondered how the social encyclicals relate to other parts of Catholic doctrine. What status do recent arguments against capital punishment, for instance, carry alongside the doctrine of Mary's immaculate conception? Which parts within these dozen or so encyclicals pertain to contingent circumstances and which parts remain timeless? All good questions.

Pope Benedict XVI's contribution came in the form of his 2009 *Caritas in Veritate* (*Charity in Truth*). In that work he attempted to clarify how social encyclicals integrate into the rest of Catholic doctrine. In it he stresses that his encyclical, like all encyclicals, should be read within the context of an organic tradition. In choosing to commemorate Pope Paul VI's 1967 *Populorum Progressio* (*On the Development of Peoples*), as he does in his opening, Benedict made clear that the theme of "integral development," so central

---

[7] For orientation to this immense body of literature, see the Pontifical Council for Justice and Peace's magisterial *Compendium of the Social Doctrine of the Church* (Vatican: Liberia Editrice Vaticana, 2005).

to Paul VI, itself has to be understood within the Church's larger doctrinal and moral framework. He writes: "It is not a case of two typologies of social doctrine, one preconciliar and one post-conciliar, differing from one another: on the contrary, there is a single teaching, consistent and at the same time ever new. . . . Coherence does not mean a closed system: on the contrary, it means dynamic faithfulness to a light received."[8]

As shepherd, Benedict here displays his characteristic humility. Particularly in the social tradition, where contingent matters are being scrutinized, a sifting process must follow. His social encyclical should be viewed in the light of others. His specific recommendations—economic policies, aid programs, government interventions—have all to be interpreted against the backdrop of established Church teaching.

Over the last century and more, Catholic social teaching has established itself as a potent tool for dialog and evangelization; but the impetus came first from Leo. For these labors and more, when Leo XIII died at the turn of the century, though the Papal States had been irretrievably lost, to those outside and inside the Church the luster of the papacy had been partially restored. After Leo XIII, a sequence of competent and, in some cases, brilliant popes would follow in his train. All would bring gifts of their own.

~~~

Unlike Leo, Pope Pius X (r. 1903–14) came from peasant stock. As a Prince of the Church, he reorganized canon

---

8 Benedict XVI, *Caritas in Veritate* (2005), 12.
~~~

law, promoted Gregorian chant, opened Holy Communion to children, performed several miracles, and would be enrolled in the Church's list of saints. After him, Pope Benedict XV tried but failed to halt the outbreak of World War I. Pope Pius XI more broadly internationalized the hierarchy—consecrating, for instance, six Chinese bishops in 1926, Indian bishops, and, for the first time ever, a bishop from Japan. Alas, by 1939 Europe would once again return to war.

In recent years, much interest has been directed toward the record of Eugenio Pacelli's reign (1939–58). As Pius XII, he, too, worked tirelessly to restore the world to peace. He failed not because of a lack of courage. Once, while papal nuncio in Munich, he personally stared down, and caused to cower in retreat, a group of armed thugs who intended to loot the papal offices. Once war broke out, however, and the plan of Hitler's exterminations became known, Pius XII orchestrated the rescue of more Jews than any other leader in Europe. Indeed, at the end of the war, Rome's chief rabbi, Israel Zoller in 1945 paid Pius XII what must at least be construed as the indirect compliment of converting to Catholicism. It's hard to imagine a rabbi taking such a step if he believed the Church's chief pastor had been in any way complicit with the Nazis. And yet, since a 1963 play called *The Deputy*, written by Rolf Hochhuth (a former member of the Hitler Youth), a series of campaigns have tried to depict the pope as just that: a complicit politician who supported the Nazis in his bid to protect the narrow interests of the Roman Church.

A number of meticulously researched books have since shown the outrageousness of such accusations.[9] Certainly such smears would never have convinced those who saw Pius's efforts first hand. During the war, Western powers collaborated with Pius in the struggle against a common foe. From the reams of documentary evidence, I offer one anecdote. In the weeks after the outbreak of the war, Pius XII released his first encyclical, *Summi Pontificatus* (*On the Unity of Human Society*). This document explicitly attacked the racial theories of the fascists. Europe's turn from God, he warned, had led its leaders to abandon even the "fundamentals of morality"; chief among these elements, the pope pointed out, is mankind's "universal brotherhood." Regardless of race, all men share a common origin. Despite legitimate differences born of ethnicity and culture, we each share a heavenly father, reason, and the duty to show charity to every man, "to whatever people they belong." Then, in an explicit snub against the Nazi race policy, the encyclical went on to emphasize that the Catholic Church herself is "neither Gentile, nor Jew."[10]

Both the Nazis and the Allies at the time of publication were clear about Pius's intention. Heinrich Mueller, head of the Gestapo, for one, declared that the encyclical was "directed exclusively against Germany, both in ideology and in regard to the German-Polish dispute." A *New York*

---

9 Among them see Rabbi David G. Dalin's *The Myth of Hitler's Pope: How Pope Pius XII Rescued Jews From the Nazis* (Washington, D.C.: Regnery Press, 2005) and Pierre Blet's *Pius XII and the Second World War According to the Archives of the Vatican* (Mahwah, NJ: Paulist Press, 1999).

10 Pius XII, *Summi Pontificatus* (1939), 15, 35, 47.

Times front-page headline on October 28, 1939 read: "Pope Condemns Dictators, Treaty Violators, Racism." Allied planes dropped eighty-eight thousand copies of Pius's text over Germany in an effort to raise resistance against the Third Reich.[11]

After the war, Pius XII also involved himself in the reconstruction of Europe and the world. One of the beautiful ways that he promoted a new humanism was in his elevation of long held belief to the status of a dogma. After a half century of atrocities, the world's image of itself had been shattered. When Pius XII declared in 1950 the dogma of the assumption of the Blessed Virgin Mary, he said it was a truth that needed to be proclaimed at this time, in part, that men may be "more convinced of the value of human life"; against materialism, he proposed that, through Mary's example, "all may see clearly to what a lofty goal our bodies and souls are destined."[12] The declaration of Mary's assumption can be partially seen, then, as a discerning exercise in reading the signs of the times. After Pius XII, another pope would call a council that asked the whole Church to do the same.

~~~

Almost no one who lived through the Second Vatican Council was satisfied by its results. One is tempted to sketch caricatures. Those on the "left" generally look back with a wistful nostalgia at the heady days of 1968 when anything seemed possible for the future Church; the first years

---

[11] See Dalin, *The Myth of Hitler's Pope*, 73.

[12] Pius XII, *Munificentissimus Deus* (1950), 42.
~~~

after the council seemed so full of promise, and more than promise, as the outlines for their aspirations seemed to be gaining flesh and living color in the six-stringed guitars and freshly-unveiled sisters that began to glide back and forth across the sanctuaries before them. Those on the "right" bemoan the loss of Corpus Christi processions, groomed altar servers, and homilies that echo the creed. For all its subsequent disappointments, one fact that both sides fail to appreciate enough, it seems to me, is the great aplomb of the pope who set the council in motion.

When Pope St. John XXIII (1958–63) called the council, he did so from a position of relative strength. Consider these recent gains. The Church had now successfully implanted herself in every continent. Catholicism had rendered itself comfortably, irrevocably, indigenous in South America, much of Africa, and parts of Asia and India. At home, in Europe, the Catholic Church had lived through the terrors of the French Revolution plus two world wars and emerged stronger; she was poised for a battle to the death against Atheistic Communism from which she would soon arise as victor. She had even begun to occupy positions of influence in traditionally Protestant nations, like Britain and America.

So much at the level of culture. At the level of dogma, no outstanding issues called out for resolution. The Church had fought hard against the isms of the age. Over the past one hundred years, popes had launched blazing condemnations against everything from relativism (*Quanta Cura*, Pius IX) to socialism (*Rerum Novarum*, Leo XIII) to Americanism (*Testem Benevolentiae Nostrae*, Leo XIII) to modernism (*Pascendi Dominici Gregis*, Pius X) to marital laxism

(*Casti Connubii*, Pius XI) to Nazism (*Mit Brennender Serge*, Pius XI), Communism (*Divini Redomptoris*, Pius XI), and unprincipled liturgical pluralism (*Mediator Dei*, Pius XII). The season had arrived for another approach. This at least was the mind of Pope John XXIII.

In his opening speech of 11 October 1962, John highlighted his hopes for the great event. Like every council before, this one would aim to make doctrine "taught more efficaciously." Nothing new here. What was novel were the limits and approach of the occasion. Unlike during the fight against Arianism in the fourth century and Luthernism in the sixteenth century, what was needed was not "a discussion of one article or another of the fundamental doctrine of the Church." The council would be pastoral in ambition and dialogical in approach; instead of issuing anathemas, it would make use, he said, of "the medicine of mercy."[13] Nowhere were the council's ambitions made more manifest than in its Pastoral Constitution on the Modern World, *Gaudium et spes*.

Gaudium et spes truly does read like a conversation. Its sixty-eight paragraphs take up a potpourri of topics from love and marriage to communications technology to the arms race and the proper role of government to contemporary evangelization. Those positive gains in technology and philosophy that could be praised were named. The genuine goods of modern civilization, the bishops argued, found their source, or at least affirmation, in the Christian story.

The compendious nature of the document was both its strength and its weakness. It could be read variously. It was

[13] John XXIII, "Opening Address to the Second Vatican Council," 11 October 1962.

only after twenty years of confusion that clarity began to return. In 1985 an extraordinary synod took up, finally, the question of the correct implementation of the council. At that event both John Paul II and Cardinal Ratzinger pointed to a theological center of the document, and even of the council. The lens through which *Gaudium et spes* should be understood, they argued, was to be found in paragraph 22. The modern world poses questions. Some of these are questions for Christians too. But not every question names a mystery. The Church also proposes answers. The answer that most needs to be heard is in fact not a statement but a person: "only in the mystery of the incarnate Word does the mystery of man take on light." Here, in the revelation of Christ, the Father "reveals man to man himself"; here is the source of light and heat that the Church can shine on a world buried under the shadows of doubt and confusion; here is the spring of truth, Truth itself, towards which all philosophies grope and before whom every knee shall bend.

Other parts of the document proved less satisfying. The most contentious paragraphs of the text, and the ones which Ratzinger himself thought ill formed, were those that dealt with the relation between nature and grace and with the so-called autonomy of earthly affairs. Paragraph 36 reads in part: "If by the autonomy of earthly affairs we mean that created things and societies themselves enjoy their own laws and values which must be gradually deciphered, put to use, and regulated by men, then it is entirely right to demand that autonomy. Such is not merely required by modern man, but harmonizes also with the will of the Creator."

After the council it became clear that such language could be taken in different directions and be used to affirm sometimes more sometimes less desirable conclusions. For one thing, the language of autonomy leans rather heavily upon the unreliable shoulders of German idealism. It was the conscientiously secular philosopher Immanuel Kant (1724–1804) who first introduced the notion of autonomy into contemporary discourse. The term itself comes from two Greek words, *auto* ("self") and *nomos* ("law"). Hence, to be autonomous is to be a law unto oneself. In Kant's view, to submit to any other law is to violate human dignity; it is to remain inauthentic and immature.[14]

Could the bishops baptize autonomy? Was the Church now to entrust the entire order of politics and moral deliberation to social scientists and democratic elections? Some theologians, like Cardinal Kasper, seemed to interpret the passage along Kantian lines. Commenting on *Gaudium et spes*, Kasper affirmed that the council initiated a new era in the Church; he has said, for example, that the "Church's recognition of the autonomy of secular fields of activity" meant that she had accepted the "fundamental concept of the modern age"; henceforth "secular matters are to be decided in a secular fashion, political matters in a political fashion, economic matters in an economic fashion."[15] Cardinal Kasper's later recommendations on Holy Communion for civilly divorced and re-married Catholics gives

[14] A theme set out in Kant's 1784 manifesto *What is Enlightenment?*

[15] Kasper, *Faith and the Future* (London: Burns and Oats, 1985), 4; cited in Roland, *Ratzinger's Faith*, 35–36.

some indication of where the uncritical elevation of autonomy lands.[16]

There are, of course, other ways of reading *Gaudium et spes*. One of them is to interpret sentences in the context of their paragraphs. In the case above, only a few sentences down the text clarifies that if "independence" is to mean created things *do not* depend on God or that man can "use them without reference to the creator," such a view is "false." Another technique is to interpret a text in the light of the Church's larger tradition. Assuming the first rule, what has been championed explicitly by John Paul II and Benedict XVI is the second strategy, which now goes by the name of the "hermeneutic of continuity."[17] New statements have to be understood in the context of old affirmations. The Church remains one and the same as she travels through time; doctrines may indeed develop, but they can never erupt from nowhere. In any case, the question of the autonomy of the secular sphere and the status of tradition

---

16 See further Kasper's *The Gospel of the Family* (Mahwah, NJ: Paulist Press, 2014), which contains his lecture to an extraordinary consistory of cardinals in preparation for the 2014–15 synods on the family; Fr. Robert Dodaro, O.S.A., brings together a series of critical, scholarly, replies to Kasper in *Remaining in the Truth of Christ: Marriage and Communion in the Catholic Church* (San Francisco: Ignatius Press, 2014). A summary of Kasper's published judgments after the synod can be found at Jan Bentz, "Cardinal Kasper: Can the 'remarried' now receive communion? 'Yes. Period,'" 24 October 2016, Lifesitenews.com.

17 Benedict XVI first popularized the term during a 2005 address to the Roman Curia, which, incidentally, Francis specifically endorsed in a letter celebrating the 450th anniversary of the Council of Trent (19 November 2013), http://press.vatican.va/content/salastampa/en/bollettino/pubblico/2013/11/23/0775/01743.html.

were both thrown open almost as soon Pope Paul VI closed the final session of the council on December 8, 1965.

~~~

There is much about the reign of Pope Paul VI (1963–78) that is not remembered. Few recall how he, too, further internationalized the College of Cardinals, or how he helped bring an end to the Vietnam War by brokering a secret meeting between the two superpowers (Nikita Kruschev was in this sense wrong when he remarked, "What the Pope has done for peace will go down in history"),[18] or how he sold the papal tiara or announced that the bones discovered under St. Peter's belonged to none other than the Apostle himself. Everyone remembers Paul VI because of *Humanae Vitae*.

"Pope Bans Pill." Any subtle arguments the text advanced—on the defense of life from conception, on the dignity of sexual love, on the mercy of the Church—were absent from the twenty-second news reports that whizzed around the world after July 29, 1968. Whatever else Paul said, what was remembered was a single judgment: No. The response was immediate. What appeared to be a majority of theologians had assumed that the council had finally made peace with modernity. Alas, peace was not to be brokered. Contraception would not be blessed. Not every marital act can be fertile. But, according to the pope, no act in good faith can be rendered deliberately *sterile*.

---

18 The incident is recounted in Peter Hebblethwaite's *Paul VI: The First Modern Pope* (New York: Paulist Press, 1993), 513.
~~~

The novelty of the document is not in its message. *Humanae Vitae* simply affirms what has many times been expressed about the connection between the unitive and procreative purposes of marriage. Paul's message was prophetic. He insisted, for one, that the mechanical separation of sex from babies would drive men and women apart. What was truly novel was the reaction it provoked. This was 1968. Rebellion was the norm. Theologians minted a neologism for heresy when they invented the term "loyal dissent"; even some bishops didn't seem to want to go along with Paul's teaching. Dissent over the pill among clergy and the laity was likely as much a cause as a symptom of deeper divisions. In 1966 roughly 200 priests in the United States resigned from ministry; in the year after *Humanae Vitae* that number swelled to 750. Few priests at the time took up the message from the pulpit. Over the next twenty years, two hundred seminaries would close their doors.[19] Half a century later, some 82 percent of US Catholics would discover no moral difficulty with birth control, to say nothing of the gulf that now divides many of the faithful from the Magisterium on gay unions, divorce, or abortion.[20] For the first time in living Catholic memory, politicians and regular folk began to think of themselves as Catholics in good standing even when they snubbed the pope, even when he was simply restating a long established tradition.

---

19 For these statistics, see James T. Fisher, *Communion of Immigrants: A History of Catholics in America* (Oxford: Oxford University Press, 2002), 143.

20 See the Gallup poll study "Americans, Including Catholics, Say Birth Control is Morally OK," 22 May 2012, www.gallup.com.

Of course, some of these trends have begun to reverse. New seminaries have opened their doors, and some old ones are filling up again. Several religious orders have seen fantastic growth in recent years. The so-called "JPII" generation of clergy and lay people has begun to assume leadership of parishes, schools, and colleges. John Paul II's development of themes from *Humanae Vitae* into the cluster of teachings now known as the "theology of the body" have helped innumerable Catholics embrace the Church's positive message of self-giving love. As secular society descends further into a degrading decadence, over the coming decades these fruits of Paul VI's message—gifts of truth to the Church and the world—so courageously defended in his final years of ministry, will continue to shine out all the more brilliantly.

~~~

In the Church's dialogue with the world in the history after Vatican II, it was not so much academic philosophy or theology that shifted as the entire culture of the West. The terms of an uneasy agreement altered. Where prior to 1968 the Church in the West could assume that Protestants, Catholics, and even skeptics stood upon a common platform of what we might call "merely cultural Christianity," after the council the scaffolding that allowed the parties to meet eye to eye, fell away. No longer do such basic goods as the protection of innocent life, religious freedom, and the sanctity of marriage win common assent among the decent fathers and the hard-working single mothers that gather around soccer fields Saturday mornings to watch
~~~

their child at play. Who knows where the new "normal" will settle. Thou shalt not fail to recycle?

The retreat of religion from our routines has produced some strange consequences. One of these is that if you wish to preserve your faith, more and more, Christians are becoming either more simplistic or more scholarly in their approach to life. The muddling main line Protestant churches and their Catholic equivalents have all spun into terminal decline. Fundamentalism, however, is holding its own. So too are those parts of the Evangelical and Catholic worlds that have embraced rigorously traditional approaches to theology and piety. Whatever we are to say about how faith can be transmitted to the next generation, the ethnic ties that once bound people to traditional religion have snapped. The fate of Quebec, Canada, offers the most dramatic instance of this failure of transmission in North America. Ireland's swift fall stands as a sobering example from Europe. Even in the United States, on a given Sunday these days you are more likely to find a Catholic in Wal-Mart than in a pew. Except for small pockets, the destruction of vibrant Catholic cultures in once traditionally Christian countries is now complete.

Where to go from here? That is a question noble souls must directly face. But any recovery, it seems to me, must begin by facing first a paradox. Catholicism is no sect. It cannot content itself by appealing merely to liturgical aesthetes or to Latinists or to the instincts of first generation Polish and Mexican immigrants. By constitution the creed is universal. Like an elegant vine, the Church seeks to wrap itself around every corner of our lives. In order to fully express itself, the Church must infect culture, implanting within the City of Man hope for the in-breaking City of God. And yet, neither can the Church simply rely on a host culture to carry its message. Spain may not exist in one hundred years, but the Church will still exist; the European Union may collapse, but the company of saints will carry on. The Church in the twenty-first century will have to wrestle once more with learning to live both in the world but not of it. Neither total immersion into culture nor an easy retreat into ghettos will satisfy.

This new fact of the near obliteration of cultural Catholicism set the agenda for the pontificates of John Paul II, of Benedict XVI, of Francis, and presumably will continue to do so for pontificates deep into the present century. Today it is not so much territories that need to be won for Christ as hearts and minds and bodies, most likely one at a time. If these efforts are to succeed, if the New Evangelization launched by St. John Paul II is to bear fruit, economic and social "structures" must once again be transformed. Catechesis will need to be stiffened. But the first fruits of success in the modern mission field, I suggest, will be seen in how we treat our bodies.

We are told that we've passed through the space age and now travel in the digital era. Man's materiality stands as the last barrier to his mastery over nature. In our gnostic age of disembodied text messaging and electronic communities, of fast food dining and overconsumption, it is an *experience* of the first truths of a religious life—of an ordered pattern of worship, of intense friendship, of pilgrimage, of fasting, of family prayer, of holy leisure—that will mark the signs of revival in our midst. Catholic Christianity is an incarnate religion. The Church's central mystery begins in the womb of a woman and is perpetuated by sharing a scared meal. After 1968, where the Church lost her rank and file was not so much in the realm of ideas—although Pater Nosters and the Creed were eventually forgotten; where the Church failed to maintain influence was in the theatre of daily life, over the rituals of bread breaking, of love making, and of earning an honest wage.

~~~

The lasting gift that the popes of the previous hundred or so years have offered to the West is a renewed opportunity for conversion. This is what the Church means by the "New Evangelization." For the New Evangelization is new only to men who have grown old and tired in their skepticism, weary and wearing in their selfishness. Circumstances change, the conditions under which faith must develop alters, but the cross abides and the creed remains the same even when our grasp of its implications for thought and life must grow. The reconciliation of faith and reason, the revival of subsidiarity, the fight against totalitarianism, the defense of religious liberty, the opening to ecumenism, stand out among some of the more fruitful gifts of the popes in recent times. Perhaps more than any of these, though, and the gift whose potential has yet to be realized is the Church's teaching on the goods of the body. I close these historical reflections by briefly naming three spheres in need of transformation by what has been called the Theology of the Body, an ancient cluster of doctrines revived and reproposed in an original fashion in John Paul
~~~

II's collection of weekly general audiences between September 1979 and November 1984.[21]

The first sphere of conflict is at the hips. Criticism against Pope Paul VI's encyclical was perhaps inevitable. Where the Church's leadership devastatingly failed was not so much in the academy as it was in the confessional and the pulpit. Pastors left the taunt of the liberal moralizers unchallenged. The world said the Church opposed sex; in truth, the Church remains the last institution still defending humane intimacy. The world said the Church thwarted love; in truth, the Church stands among the few forces fighting for lasting friendship. The world said that the Church halted progress; in truth, she guards the glorious memory of God's word that pronounced us male and female against the transhumanists that would condemn all biology to history. Instead of tying the marital act into the cosmic purposes of Christ for the salvation of the world, we let the libertines drain carnal love of its significance.

The scattered carnage of the sexual revolution lies now in plain view. Sexual pleasure released from the responsibilities of marriage soon abandons its service in search of less honorable rewards. The sign that your twenty-five-year-old son has finally come of age is, these days, as likely to be marked by an engagement to a woman as by the announcement that he and his girlfriend are bringing home a new Golden Retriever. The fruit of Christian faith is hope in the future. As we repudiate faith, hope also begins to fail, and along with it the energy needed to sustain those adult

---

21 First collected in English under the title *The Theology of the Body: Human Love in the Divine Plan* (Boston: Pauline, 1997).

commitments that demand self-sacrifice, such as raising children. The consequence of reducing the morality of sex to the arrangements of consenting adults is that disorders of the bedroom now threaten to overturn not merely the stability of households but also the character of entire nations.

Another kind of effort must be directed above the belt, in the gut. All religions regulate food. It is folly to think that Catholicism will matter if it doesn't also make demands on the stomach. Fish Friday was about more than the simple fast. It provided a cord that bound otherwise strangers together into a common witness of faith. I recall my first experience of a banquet at a Catholic university. The community was small; the administration presided by a Catholic priest. Our meal fell on a Friday. Given the amount of hamburger that was thrown at us, it was almost as though, by flaunting the once common custom, the administration was trying to emphasize how inclusive it had become. I suppose everyone except the Catholics felt welcome. In any case, in the older dispensation the Catholics at the after-work party could be *seen*. They may have drunk more whiskey than their Protestant colleagues, and perhaps been less sober, but at least they didn't touch the beef. In some places, particularly where Islam has become a contentious rival for new converts—as in Britain—bishops have reinstated the discipline of a public abstinence throughout the year. Let us hope that similar restorations can take place before simple prudence becomes a matter of naked necessity.

And finally, there is the wallet. In the United States the so-called "blue laws" restricted, and in some places still limit, the kinds of shopping people can do on Sundays. Beyond an increase in frantic activity, and fatigue, and restlessness, and excess, the loss of Sunday has resulted in the loss of the sense of sacred time. Our Lord is jealous. If our particular country no longer respects the Sabbath, Catholics must learn again to conform themselves to the habits of a better country and labor until the law once more mirrors God's love for sacred rest. Catholics are to fight to restore the Sabbath as a public holiday. As the *Catechism* puts it rather provocatively: "In respecting religious liberty and the common good of all, Christians should seek recognition of Sundays and the Church's holy days as legal holidays."[22]

~~~

In these pages we have witnessed in broad strokes the outline of the grand masterpiece that is the Church's influence upon Western history and sensibilities, of gifts imparted, whether remembered or not, through faithful martyrs, philosophers, and scientists; in our politics, our universities, and our missions; and by mystics and by popes in their struggle to proclaim the Gospel amidst changing circumstances. In volume 2, we delve deeper into some of the details. Our reflections in a forthcoming volume will follow not a historical narrative but a thematic approach and will chart particular expressions of culture the Church has produced and consider possibilities for the culture it may yet transform.

Having myself now travelled through these past two thousand years of Catholicism's influence upon the West with you, I close this first volume with the words of another

---

22 CCC 2188.
~~~

convert. When Robert Hugh Benson, a sophisticated Anglican clergyman, after a long sojourn, first entered Rome and the faith which animates that city, he saw at last the place from which he could stand and see the world aright. This is the world that every believer is beckoned to discover. With all the joy and wonder of a child who has awoke from a long night of fever, we, too, can learn to recognize the gifts of the Church that surround us and enrich us all. It is into this waking day that I invite you, dear reader, as we travel still farther together in the volume to come.

> Thus, in truth, a sojourn in Rome means an expansion of view that is beyond words. Whereas up to that time I had been accustomed to image Christianity to myself as a delicate flower, divine because of its supernatural fragility, now I saw that it was a tree in whose branches the fowls of the air, once the enemies of its tender growth, can lodge in security—divine since the wideness of its reach and the strength of its mighty roots can be accounted for by nothing else. Before I had thought of it as of a fine, sweet aroma, to be appreciated apart; now I saw that it was the leaven, hid in the heavy measures of the world, expressing itself in terms incalculably coarser than itself, until the whole is leavened.[23]

---

23 Robert Hugh Benson, *Confessions of a Convert* (London: Longmans, Green, and Co., 1913), chapter 8.3.

SELECT BIBLIOGRAPHY

Aristotle. *Nicomachean Ethics*. Translated by T. Irwin. Indianapolis, IN: Hackett, 1999.

———. *Politics*. Translated by B. Jowett. In *The Collected Works of Aristotle, The Revised Oxford Translation*. Edited by Jonathan Barnes. New Jersey: Princeton University Press, 1984.

———. *Metaphysics*. Translated by W. D. Ross. In *The Collected Works of Aristotle, The Revised Oxford Translation.* Edited by Jonathan Barnes. New Jersey: Princeton University Press, 1984.

Armstrong, Karen. *Holy War: The Crusades and Their Impact on Today's World.* New York: Random House, 2001.

Arndt and Gingrich. *A Greek –English Lexicon of the New Testament and Other Early Christian Literature.* Chicago: University of Chicago Press, 1952.

Barett, William. *World Christian Encyclopedia.* Oxford: Oxford University Press, 2001.

Blet, Pierre. *Pius XII and the Second World War According to the Archives of the Vatican.* Mahwah, NJ: Paulist Press, 1999.

Boland, Vivian. *St. Thomas Aquinas*. London: Continuum, 2007.

Bongars. *Gesta Dei per Francos*. In *A Source Book for Medieval History*. Edited by Oliver J. Thatcher and Edgar Holmes McNeal. New York: Scribners, 1905.

Brown, Dan. *The Da Vinci Code: A Novel*. New York: Anchor Books, 2003.

Cassian, John. *The Conferences*. Translated by B. Ramsey. Mahwah, NJ: Paulist Press, 1997.

Catalogus Monasteriorum O.S.B. Romae: SS. Patriarchae Benedicti Familiae Confoederatae, 2010.

Chadwick, Owen. *The Penguin History of the Reformation of the Church*. London: Penguin, 1990.

Clark, Kenneth. *Civilisation: A Personal View*. New York: Harper and Row, 1969.

Courtois, Stephen, ed. *The Black Book of Communism: Crimes, Terror, Repression*. Cambridge, Mass: Harvard University Press, 1999.

Crocker, H. W. *Triumph: The Power and the Glory of the Catholic Church*. New York: Crown Forum, 2003.

Crombie, Alistair. *Medieval and Early Modern Science*. 2 vols. New York: Doubleday, 1959.

Dalin, David G. *The Myth of Hitler's Pope: How Pope Pius XII Rescued Jews From the Nazis*. Washington, DC: Regnery Press, 2005.

Daniel-Rops, H. *Cathedral and Crusade: Studies of the Medieval Church 1050-1350*. Translated by John Warrington. London: J. M. Dent and Sons, 1957.

Davidson, Ian. *Voltaire: A Life.* New York: Pegasus Books, 2010.

Dawkins, Richard. *A River out of Eden: A Darwinian View of Life.* New York: Basic Books, 2008.

Dawson, Christopher. *The Crisis of Western Education.* Washington, DC: Catholic University of America Press, 2010.

Di Vitoria. *De iure belli relectio.* In *Vitoria: Political Writings*. Edited and translated by A. Pagden and J. Lawrance. Cambridge: Cambridge University Press, 1991.

Dodaro, Robert, ed. *Remaining in the Truth of Christ: Marriage and Communion in the Catholic Church.* San Francisco: Ignatius Press, 2014.

Durán, Diego. *The History of the Indies of New Spain.* Translated by Doris Heyden. London: University of Oklahoma Press, 1994.

Durant, Will. *The Reformation.* In *The Story of Civilization.* New York: Simon and Schuster, 1935-1975.

Erasmus, Desiderius. "Letter to Jodocus." In *Christian Humanism and the Reformation: Selected Writings of Erasmus,* edited by John C. Olin. New York: Fordham University Press, 1987.

———. *Praise of Folly*. Translated by B. Radice. London: Penguin, 1971.

Eusebius. *History of the Church*. Translated by P. Maier. Grand Rapids, MI: Kregel, 1999.

———. *Life of Constantine*. Translated by E. Richardson. In *Nicene and Post-Nicene Fathers, second series*, Vol. 1. Grand Rapids, MI: Wm. B. Eerdmans, 1955.

Farrell, Allan P., trans. *Ratio Studiorum.* Washington, DC: Conference of Major Superiors of Jesuits, 1970.

Farrow, Douglas. *Desiring a Better Country: Forays in Political Theology.* Montreal: McGill-Queens, 2015.

Fisher, James T. *Communion of Immigrants: A History of Catholics in America.* Oxford: Oxford University Press, 2002.

Foster, Benjamin, ed. and trans. *Epic of Gilgamesh.* New York: W.W. Norton & Company, 2001.

Galen. *Galen on Jews and Christians*. Edited and translated by Richard Walzer. London: OUP, 1949.

Galilei, Galileo. "Letter to Christiana." In *The Galileo Affair: A Documentary History*, edited and translated by M. Finocchiaro. Los Angeles: University of California Press, 1989.

———. *Letter* of 21 November 1613. In *Edizione nazionale delle Opere di Galileo Galilei,* dir. A. Favaro, edition of 1968, Vol. V in John Paul II, "Allocution of October 31," 1992.

Gaul, Niels. "The Manuscript Tradition." In *A Companion to the Ancient Greek Language*, edited by E. Bakker. London: Blackwell Publishing, 2010.

Gibbon, Edward. *The History of the Decline and Fall of the Roman Empire.* Edited by J. B. Bury. London: Metheun and Co., 1902.

Grant, Edward. *God and Reason in the Middle Ages.* Cambridge: Cambridge University Press, 2001.

Grebel, Conrad. "Letter to Thomas Müntzer" 5 September 1524. In *The Protestant Reformation,* edited by Hillerbrand. London: Macmillan, 1968.

Gregory the Great. *Dialogues*. Translated by Zimmerman. Washington, DC: Catholic University of America Press, 2002.

Hebblethwaite, Peter. *Paul VI: The First Modern Pope.* New York: Paulist Press, 1993.

Hippolytus. *Apostolic Tradition.* In *The Roman Breviary*, bilingual edition (1963), Vol. 1. New Jersey: University of Princeton Press, 1989.

Matthew Lamb and Matthew Levering, eds. *Vatican II: Renewal Within Tradition.* Oxford: OUP, 2008.

Holden and Pinset. *The Catholic Gift to Civilization.* London: Catholic Truth Society, 2011.

Howard, Thomas Albert. *Protestantism and the Rise of the Modern German University.* Oxford: Oxford University Press, 2006.

Hoye, William J. "The Religious Roots of Academic Freedom." In *Theological Studies* 58 (1997): 409-428.

Hugh of St. Victor. *Didascalicon: On the Study of Reading*. Translated by Taylor. New York: Columbia University Press, 1991.

Ignatius of Antioch. *Epistle to the Romans*. Translated and edited by Roberts and Donaldson In *Ante-Nicene Fathers*, Vol. 1. Buffalo, NY: Christian Literature Publishing Co., 1885.

Irenaeus. *Against Heresies*. Translated and edited by Roberts and Donaldson. In *Ante-Nicene Fathers*, Vol. 1. Buffalo, NY: Christian Literature Publishing Co., 1885.

Jedin, Hubert, ed. *History of the Church,* Vol. 1. London: Burns and Oats, 1980.

Justin Martyr. *Dialogue with Trypho*. Translated and edited by Roberts and Donaldson. In *Ante-Nicene Fathers*, Vol. 1. Buffalo, NY: Christian Literature Publishing Co., 1885.

———. *First Apology*. Translated by L. W. Barnard. Washington, DC: Catholic University Press of America, 1997.

Kasper, Walter. *Faith and the Future.* London: Burns and Oats, 1985.

———. *The Gospel of the Family.* Mahwah, NJ: Paulist Press, 2014.

Kee, Howard, Jerry Frost, Emily Albu, Carter Lindberg, and Dana Robert. *Christianity: A Social and Cultural History*. New York: Pearson, 1997.

Las Casas, Bartolomé. *A Short Account of the Destruction of the Indies*. Translated by N. Griffen. London: Penguin, 1992.

Laux, John. *Church History: A Complete History of the Catholic Church to the Present Day*. New York: Benziger Brothers, 1936.

Le Jeune, Paul. *Jesuit Missionaries to North America: Spiritual Writings and Biographical Sketches*. Translated and edited by Francois Roustang. San Francisco, CA: Ignatius Press, 2006.

Leo XIII. *Aeterni Patris* (*On the Restoration of Christian Philosophy*) August 4, 1879.

Lewis, C. S. and Giovanni Calabria. *The Latin Letters of C. S. Lewis*. South Bend, IN: St. Augustine Press, 1998.

Locke, John. *Letter on Toleration*. Edited by Tully. Indianapolis, IN: Hackett Publishing, 1986.

Luther, Martin. *Disputation Against Scholastic Theology*. In *Luther's Works*. Vol. 31, *Career of the Reformer: I*, edited by H. Grimm. Minneapolis, MN: Fortress Press, 1957.

———. *Freedom of a Christian*. Edited by Dillenberger. New York: Anchor Books, 1962.

———. *Disputation Against Scholastic Theology*. Edited by Lull and Russell. Minneapolis, MN: Fortress Press, 2012.

Machiavelli, Niccolò. *Discourses*. Translated by D. Donno. New York: Bantam Books, 1966.

Martyrdom of Polycarp. Translated and edited by Roberts and Donaldson. In *Ante-Nicene Fathers*, Vol. 1. Buffalo, NY: Christian Literature Publishing Co., 1885.

Marx, Karl. *Communist Manifesto*. Translated by Jones. London: Penguin, 1967.

Miller, D. A. "Living Among the Breakage: Contextual Theology-Making and Ex-Muslim Christians." PhD thesis at the University of Edinburgh (2014): 94-100.

Miller, D. A. and P. Johnstone. "Believers in Christ form a Muslim Background: A Global Consensus." In *Interdisciplinary Journal of Research on Religion*, Vol. 11 (2015): 1-19.

Newman, John Henry. *Historical Sketches.* London: Longmans, Green, and Co., 1906.

Nichols, Aidan. *Lovely Like Jerusalem: The Fulfilment of the Old Testament in Christ and the Church.* Ignatius: San Francisco, 2005.

O'Donovan, Oliver. *The Just War Revisited.* Cambridge: Cambridge University Press, 2003.

Percy, Walker. *The Moviegoer.* New York: Knopf, 1961.

Pliny the Younger. *Letters*. Translated by John Lewis. London: Trubner & Co., 1879.

Pontifical Council for Justice and Peace. *Compendium of the Social Doctrine of the Church.* Vatican: Liberia Editrice Vaticana, 2005.

Pope Benedict XVI. *Caritas in Veritate* (*Charity in Truth*), 25 December 2005.

———. *Spe Salvi*, 20 November 2007.

Pope Francis. *Laudato Si* (*On Care for our Common Home*), 24 May 2015.

———. "Homily at St. Peter's Square," 7 September 2013.

Pope Pius XII. *Fulgens radiator* (*On St. Benedict*), 21 March 1947.

———. *Summi Pontificatus* (*On the Unity of Human Society*), 20 October 1939.

———. *Munificentissimus Deus* (*Defining the Dogma of the Assumption*), 1 November 1950.

Pope St. John XXIII. "Opening Address to the Second Vatican Council" 11 October 1962.

Pope St. John Paul II. "Address to Young Muslims," 19 August 1985.

———. *Ut unum sint* (*On the Church's Commitment to Ecumenism*) 25 May 1995.

———. *The Theology of the Body: Human Love in the Divine Plan*. Boston: Pauline, 1997.

Ratzinger, Joseph. *'In the Beginning...': A Catholic Understanding of the Story of Creation and the Fall.* Translated by Boniface Ramsey. Grand Rapids, MI: Eerdmans, 1995.

Second Vatican Council. *Nostra Aetate* (*The Relation of the Church to Non-Christian Religions*), October 28, 1965.

Scanlon, Regis. "Did Vatican II Reverse the Church's leaching on Religious Liberty." *Homiletic and Pastoral Review* (January 2011): 61–68.

Seneca. "On Providence." In *Dialogues and Essays*, translated by John Davie. Oxford: OUP, 2008.

Sophocles. *Antigone.* In *The Three Theban Plays,* translated by Robert Fagles. London: Penguin, 1980.

Sozomen. *Ecclesiastical History*. Translated by Chester D. Hartranft. In *Post-Nicene Fathers, second series*, Vol. 2, edited by Philip Schaff and Henry Wace. Buffalo, NY: Christian Literature Publishing Co., 1892.

St. Augustine. *On Christian Teaching.* Translated by R. P. H. Green. Oxford: OUP, 1999.

St. Benedict. *Rule of St. Benedict*. Translated by W. Fahey. Charlotte, NC: TAN Books, 2013.

St. Ignatius of Loyla. *The Autobiography of St. Ignatius of Loyola.* Edited by J. F. X. O'Connor. New York: Benziger Brothers, 1900.

St. John Chrysostom. *Homily* 21 "On the Statutes to the People of Antioch." Translated by W. R. W. Stephens. In *Nicene and Post-Nicene Fathers, first series*, Vol. 9, edited by Philip Schaff. New York: Christian Literature Publishing Co., 1886.

St. Thérèse of Lisieux. *Story of a Soul: The Autobiography of St. Thérèse of Lisieux.* Translated by J. Clarke. Washington, DC: Institute of Carmelite Studies, 1997.

Stark, Rodney. *God's Battalions: The Case for the Crusades.* New York: Harper One, 2009.

Stillman, Drake. *Galileo.* New York: Hill and Wang, 1980.

Tacitus. *Annals of Imperial Rome.* Translated by A. J. Church and W. J. Brodribb. London: Macmillan and Co., 1895.

Tanner, J. Pau. "The History of Interpretation of the Song of Songs." In *Bibliotheca Sacra* 154: 613 (1997): 23-46.

Tertullian. *The Apology of Tertullian.* Translated by William Reeve. London: Griffith, Ferran, Okeden & Welsh, 1709.

The Canons and Decrees of the Council of Trent. Translated by H. J. Schroeder. Charlotte, NC: TAN Books, 2011.

The Catholic Encyclopedia. 16 Vols. New York: Robert Appleton Company, 1907-1922.

The Oxford History of Islam. Edited by John L. Esposito. Oxford: Oxford University Press, 1999.

Theodoret. *Ecclesiastical History*. Translated by B. Jackson. In *Nicene and Post-Nicene Fathers, second series*, Vol. 3, edited by Philip Schaff and Henry Wace. Buffalo, NY: Christian Literature Publishing Co., 1892.

Thorndike, Lynn, ed. *University Records and Life in the Middle Ages*. New York: Columbia University Press, 1944.

Topping, Ryan. *The Case for Catholic Education*. Kettering, OH: Angelico Press, 2015.

Tyerman, Christopher. *God's War: A New History of the Crusades*. Cambridge, MA: Harvard University Press, 2006.

Virgil. *Eclogues*. Translated by Guy Lee. London: Penguin, 1984.

Vitoria. *On the American Indians*. Translated by A. Pagden and J. Lawrance. Cambridge: Cambridge University Press, 1992.

von Clausewitz, Carl. *On War*. Translated and edited by Howard and Paret. New Jersey: University of Princeton Press, 1989.

Voltaire. *Portable Philosophical Dictionary.* In Voltaire, *Candide and Related Texts*, translated by David Wootton. Indianapolis, IN: Hackett, 2000.

Weigel, George. *God's Choice: Pope Benedict XVI and the Future of the Catholic Church.* New York: HarperCollins Publisher, 2005.

———. *Witness to Hope: The Biography of Pope John Paul II.* New York: Harper Collins, 1999.

Woods, Thomas. *How the Catholic Church Built Western Civilization.* Washington, DC: Regnery Publishing, 2005.

Zosimus. *New History.* Translated by R. T. Ridley. Canberra: Australian Association for Byzantine Studies, 1982.

IMAGE CREDITS

"Monuments of Nineveh, Second Series" plate 5, London, J. Murray, 1853, editor Austen Henry Layard , drawing by L. Gruner. Public domain via Wikimedia Commons.

Dante and Virgil in Hell, oil on canvas (1850), Bouguereau, William-Adolphe (1825-1905), Musée d'Orsay, France. Public domain via Wikimedia Commons.

Nero's Torches (Christian Candlesticks), oil on canvas (1876), Siemiradzki, Henryk (1843-1902), National Museum Kraków, Poland. Public domain via Wikimedia Commons.

Battle of Milvian Bridge, oil on panel (17th century), Rubens, Peter Paul (1577-1640), The Wallace Collection, England, Public domain via Wikimedia Commons.

Saint Ambrose barring Theodosius I from Milan Cathedral, oil on canvas (1619-1620), van Dyck, Anthony (1599-1641), National Gallery, England. Public domain via Wikimedia Commons.

St. Scholastica's Abbey, Subiaco, Italy (photo) / Bridgeman Images.

Oxford Syline, England (photo), Bames, Keith / Shutterstock

The Ghent Altarpiece, oil on oak panel (circa 1430-1432), van Eyck, Jan, and van Eyck, Hubert. St. Bravo's Cathedral, Belgium. Public domain via Wikimedia Commons.

Battle between Crusaders and Moslems, from Le Roman de Godefroi de Bouillon (vellum), French School, (14th century) / Bibliotheque Nationale, Paris, France / Bridgeman Images.

Portrait of Henry VIII, oil on canvas (1537-1547), Hans Holbein the Younger. Walker Art Gallery, England. Public domain via Wikimedia Commons.

Portrait of Martin Luther, oil on panel (1528), Lucas Cranach the Elder (1472-1553), Veste Coburg, Germany. Public domain via Wikimedia Commons.

The Crucifixion of Saint Peter, oil on canvas (1600-1601), Caravaggio, Cerasi Chapel, Italy. Public domain via Wikimedia Commons.

Il Gesu, Italy (photo). Evgeny Mogilnikov / Shutterstock.

Convent of San Esteban, Spain (photo). Farbregas Hareluya / Shutterstock.

Stained glass window of St. Kateri Tekakwitha (photo). Nancy Bauer / Shutterstock.

St. Isaac Jogues. Public domain via Wikimedia Commons.

Liberty Guiding the People, oil on canvas (1830), Delacroix, Eugène (1798-1863). Louvre Museum, France. Public domain via Wikimedia Commons.

Portrait of John Locke, Kneller, Godfrey. Photograph of painting by Stephen Dickson. National Portrait Gallery, England. Public domain via Wikimedia Commons.

Sainte Therese de Lisieux / Photo © Collection Gregoire / Bridgeman Images.

Members of the Royal 22e Regiment in audience with Pope Pius XII. July 4, 1944. Canada. Dept. of National Defence. Public domain via Wikimedia Commons.

Gdansk, 1987. Pope John Paul II's third Pilgrimage to Poland. / Forum / Bridgeman Images.